The Writings of Frithjof Schuon
Series

World Wisdom
The Library of Perennial Philosophy

The Library of Perennial Philosophy is dedicated to the exposition of the timeless Truth underlying the diverse religions. This Truth, often referred to as the *Sophia Perennis*—or Perennial Wisdom—finds its expression in the revealed Scriptures as well as in the writings of the great sages and the artistic creations of the traditional worlds.

The Perennial Philosophy provides the intellectual principles capable of explaining both the formal contradictions and the transcendent unity of the great religions.

Ranging from the writings of the great sages of the past to the perennialist authors of our time, each series of our Library has a different focus. As a whole, they express the inner unanimity, transforming radiance, and irreplaceable values of the great spiritual traditions.

Light on the Ancient Worlds appears as one of our selections in the Writings of Frithjof Schuon series.

The Writings of Frithjof Schuon

The Writings of Frithjof Schuon form the foundation of our library because he is the pre-eminent exponent of the Perennial Philosophy. His work illuminates this perspective in both an essential and comprehensive manner like none other.

Books by Frithjof Schuon

The Transcendent Unity of Religions
Spiritual Perspectives and Human Facts
Gnosis: Divine Wisdom
Language of the Self
Stations of Wisdom
Understanding Islam
Light on the Ancient Worlds
In the Tracks of Buddhism
Treasures of Buddhism
Logic and Transcendence
Esoterism as Principle and as Way
Castes and Races
Sufism: Veil and Quintessence
From the Divine to the Human
Christianity/Islam: Essays on Esoteric Ecumenicism
Survey of Metaphysics and Esoterism
In the Face of the Absolute
The Feathered Sun: Plains Indians in Art and Philosophy
To Have a Center
Roots of the Human Condition
Images of Primordial and Mystic Beauty: Paintings by Frithjof Schuon
Echoes of Perennial Wisdom
The Play of Masks
Road to the Heart: Poems
The Transfiguration of Man
The Eye of the Heart
Songs for a Spiritual Traveler: Selected Poems
Form and Substance in the Religions
Adastra and Stella Maris: Poems by Frithjof Schuon

Edited Writings of Frithjof Schuon

The Essential Writings of Frithjof Schuon, ed. Seyyed Hossein Nasr
The Fullness of God: Frithjof Schuon on Christianity,
ed. James S. Cutsinger
Prayer Fashions Man: Frithjof Schuon on the Spiritual Life,
ed. James S. Cutsinger

Light on
the Ancient Worlds

A New Translation with Selected Letters

by

Frithjof Schuon

Includes Other Previously
Unpublished Writings

Edited by Deborah Casey

World Wisdom

Light on the Ancient Worlds:
A New Translation with Selected Letters
© 2006 World Wisdom, Inc.

Translated by Deborah Casey, Mark Perry, Jean-Pierre Lafouge
and James S. Cutsinger

Published in French as
Regards sur les mondes anciens
Editions traditionnelles, Paris, 1980.

Library of Congress Cataloging-in-Publication Data

Schuon, Frithjof, 1907-1998
  [Regards sur les mondes anciens. English]
  Light on the ancient worlds : a new translation : with selected letters / by
Frithjof Schuon ; edited by Deborah Casey.
p. cm. – (The writings of Frithjof Schuon) (The library of perennial philosophy)
Translated by Deborah Casey et al.
Includes bibliographical references and index.
ISBN-13: 978-0-941532-72-3 (pbk. : alk. paper)
ISBN-10: 0-941532-72-0 (pbk. : alk. paper)   1. Religion–Philosophy. I. Casey,
Deborah, 1951- II. Schuon, Frithjof, 1907- Correspondence. English.
Selections. III. Title. IV. Series.

BL51.S4656513 2006
200–dc22

                                              2005024843

Cover Art: Pectoral in the shape of a falcon from the tomb
of King Tutankhamun, Egypt, 1333-1324 B.C.

Printed on acid-free paper in Canada.

For information address World Wisdom, Inc.
P. O. Box 2682, Bloomington, Indiana 47402-2682

www.worldwisdom.com

CONTENTS

Editor's Preface

The title *Light on the Ancient Worlds* may at first seem obvious to many readers of the twenty-first century. We have in mind those who reflexively think of humanity as blazing a trail of ever-unfolding progress and who are convinced that people of today look out as from a very lofty and privileged eminence upon vistas never before beheld by mankind. Such a viewpoint will be brought up short in reading: "Contemporary man has collected a great mass of experiences and is therefore rather disillusioned, but the conclusions he draws from it are so false that they virtually reduce to nothing all that has been gained, or ought to have been gained."[1] If it is not the discoveries and insights of the modern age that elucidate the past, then one may well wonder what this "light" is and where it comes from?

The essays presented here all speak to this question. They do so by enunciating the spiritual patrimony, not of the humanity of any particular time or place, but of man as such in light of Truth as such. This patrimony has been variously called in the West, the "perennial philosophy" (*philosophia perennis*) or the "perennial religion" (*religio perennis*), and it corresponds to the *Sanâtana Dharma* of the Vedantists.

When the first French edition of this book was published in 1967, Frithjof Schuon's reputation as the pre-eminent contemporary spokesman of the perennial philosophy was already well established. More than 30 titles from his pen have now appeared in English, covering such topics as metaphysics, philosophy, comparative religion, symbolism, aesthetics, and the nature of the human state. During his lifetime, Schuon's works won respect from both prominent scholars and spiritual authorities, and they have always found an audience among serious readers looking for a viewpoint free from the shallow academic categories, the relativism, and the "psychologism" that dominate the modern outlook. Following his death in 1998, his writings remain unequaled in setting forth the principles of perennialist thought as well as their applications.

---

[1] In the chapter "Naiveté", p. 84.

It is for this reason that World Wisdom has undertaken a new edition of this classic work, including a fully revised translation of the text. In the interest of remaining as close as possible to the original book, the chapter arrangement of the initial French edition has been restored. Some new elements have also been added. Schuon's breadth of erudition is vast, his use of words precise, his prose both multi-dimensional and synthetic. One sentence may touch upon several crucial notions—often conveyed by phrases from Sanskrit, Latin, Greek, and Arabic—and these key ideas frequently appear in other articles. For those unaccustomed to reading philosophical books or approaching his writings for the first time, assimilating this richness and exactitude can prove difficult. Thus, as an aid to readers, an Index and a Glossary of foreign terms and phrases have been included.

The most notable addition is an Appendix of selections from previously unpublished material. Throughout his life, Schuon wrote many brief texts that were available only privately, and thus to a limited number of readers. He also wrote hundreds of letters, mainly in response to questions both from people whom he was never to meet and from those he knew well. These private works often contain the seeds of ideas that were later developed into articles; they also serve to illustrate, emphasize, or comment upon subjects treated at length in his published writings. The passages presented here have been chosen not because they were the particular "historical" antecedents of the following chapters, but simply with a view to opening for readers a new and very rich dimension in the Schuon opus.

Deborah Casey

Light on the Ancient Worlds

The whole existence of the peoples of antiquity, and of traditional peoples in general, is dominated by two key-ideas, the idea of Center and the idea of Origin. In the spatial world where we live, every value is related in some way to a sacred Center, which is the place where Heaven has touched the earth; in every human world there is a place where God has manifested Himself in order to pour forth His grace. And it is the same for the Origin, which is the quasi-timeless moment when Heaven was near and terrestrial things were still half-celestial; but in the case of civilizations having a historical founder, it is also the period when God spoke, thus renewing the primordial covenant for the branch of humanity concerned. To conform to tradition is to remain faithful to the Origin, and for this very reason it is also to place oneself at the Center; it is to dwell in the primordial Purity and the universal Norm. Everything in the behavior of ancient and traditional peoples can be explained, directly or indirectly, by reference to these two ideas, which are like landmarks in the measureless and perilous world of forms and change.

It is this kind of mythological subjectivity, if one may so express it, which makes it possible to understand the imperialism of ancient civilizations, for example, for it is not enough here to invoke the "law of the jungle", even though this law may be biologically inevitable and to that extent legitimate; one must also take account of the fact, even giving it precedence since human beings are concerned, that each ancient civilization can be said to live on a remembrance of the lost Paradise and that it presents itself—insofar as it is the vehicle of an immemorial tradition or a Revelation that restores the "lost word"—as the most direct branch of the "age of the Gods". It is therefore in every case "our people" and no other who perpetuate primordial humanity from the point of view of both wisdom and the virtues; and it must be recognized that this perspective is neither more nor less false than the exclusivism of religions or, on the purely natural plane, the empirical unicity of every ego. There are many peoples who do not call themselves by the name given them by others; they call themselves simply "the people" or "men"; other tribes are not "faithful", having separated themselves from the main

1

stem; this is *grosso modo* the point of view of the Roman Empire as well as the Confederation of the Iroquois.

The purpose of ancient imperialism was to spread an "order", a state of equilibrium and stability which conforms to a divine model and which is in any case reflected in nature, notably in the planetary world; the Roman emperor, like the monarch of the "Celestial Middle Kingdom", wields his power thanks to a "mandate from Heaven". Julius Caesar, holder of this mandate and "divine man" (*divus*),[1] was conscious of the providential range of his mission; as far as he was concerned, nothing had the right to oppose it, Vercingetorix having been for him a sort of heretic. If the non-Roman peoples were considered "barbarians", it is above all because they were outside the "order"; from the point of view of the *Pax Romana*, they manifested disequilibrium, instability, chaos, perpetual menace. In Christianity (*corpus mysticum*) and Islam (*dâr al-islâm*) the theocratic essence of the imperial idea is clearly apparent; without theocracy there could be no civilization worthy of the name; so true is this that the Roman emperors, in the midst of the pagan breakup and from the time of Diocletian, felt the need to divinize themselves or allow themselves to be divinized while improperly claiming for themselves the position of conqueror of the Gauls descended from Venus. The modern idea of "civilization" is not without a connection, historically speaking, to the traditional idea of "empire"; but the "order" has become purely human and entirely profane, as is proven in any case by the notion of "progress", which is the very negation of any celestial origin; in fact "civilization" is merely an urban refinement within the framework of a worldly and mercantile outlook, and this explains its hostility to virgin nature as well as to religion. According to the criteria of "civilization", the contemplative hermit—who represents human spirituality and at the same time the sanctity of virgin nature—can only be a sort of "savage", whereas in reality he is the earthly witness of Heaven.

---

[1] "See the man, see him of whose promised coming thou hast so often heard, Caesar Augustus, son of a God, who will found anew the Golden Age in the fields where Saturn reigned of old, and who will extend his empire even over the Garamantes and the Indians" (*Aeneid* 6:791-95). Caesar prepared a world for the reign of Christ. Note that Dante placed the murderers of Caesar in the deepest hell, together with Judas. Cf. "*Divus* Julius Caesar" by Adrian Paterson (*Études Traditionnelles*, June, 1940).

These considerations allow us to make a few remarks here concerning the complexity of authority in Western Christianity. The
emperor, in contrast to the pope, incarnates temporal power; but
more than that he also represents, by virtue of his pre-Christian
but nonetheless celestial origin,[2] an aspect of universality whereas
the pope is identified by his function with the Christian religion
alone. The Muslims in Spain were not persecuted until the clergy
had become too powerful in comparison with the temporal power;
this power, which belongs to the emperor, represents in this case
universality or "realism", and therefore "tolerance", and thus also
by the nature of things a certain element of wisdom. This ambiguity
in the imperial function—of which the emperors were conscious to
one degree or another[3]—explains in part what may be called the
traditional disequilibrium of Christianity; and it may be said that
the pope recognized this ambiguity—or this aspect of superiority
paradoxically accompanying an inferiority—by prostrating himself
before Charlemagne after his coronation.[4]

Imperialism can come either from Heaven or simply from the
earth, or again from hell; be that as it may, what is certain is that
humanity cannot remain divided into a scattering of independent
tribes; the bad would inevitably hurl themselves upon the good, and

[2] Dante has no hesitation in citing this superhuman origin in support of his doctrine of imperial monarchy.

[3] The position is clear beyond doubt in the case of Constantine as well as Charlemagne.

[4] There is a curious relationship—it may be mentioned in passing—between the
imperial function and the part played by the court jester, and this relationship
seems to be associated with the fact that the costume of jesters, like that of certain
emperors, was adorned with little bells, following the example of the sacred robe
of the High Priest; the role of the jester was originally that of saying in public what
no one else could allow himself to say, thus introducing an element of truth into
a world constrained by unavoidable conventions; now this function, whether one
wishes it or not, is reminiscent of sapience or esoterism, for in its own way it shat-
ters "forms" in the name of "the spirit that bloweth where it listeth". But folly alone
can allow itself to enunciate cruel truths and to challenge idols precisely because it
stands apart from a particular human system and this proves that in that world of
facades which is society the pure and simple truth is madness. This is doubtless why
the function of the court jester succumbed in the end to the world of formalism
and hypocrisy: the intelligent fool ended by giving way to the buffoon, who very
soon became tedious and disappeared.

the result would be a humanity oppressed by the bad and hence the worst of all imperialisms. What may be called the imperialism of the good constitutes therefore a sort of inevitable and providential preventive war; without it no great civilization is conceivable.[5] It may be argued that all this does not take us away from human imperfection, and we agree; far from advocating an illusory angelism, we acknowledge the fact that man remains always man whenever collectivities with their interests and passions are involved; the leaders of men are obliged to take account of this fact, unpleasant though it may be to those "idealists" who judge that the "purity" of a religion consists in committing suicide. And this leads us to a truth all too often lost sight of by believers themselves: namely, that religion, to the extent it is manifested collectively, necessarily relies upon something to support it in one way or another, though without losing anything of its doctrinal and sacramental content or the impartiality resulting from them; for the Church is one thing as a social organism and another as a divine repository, which remains by definition outside the entanglements and constraints of human nature, whether individual or collective. To wish to modify the terrestrial roots of the Church—roots for which the phenomenon of sanctity amply compensates—is to end by debasing religion in its very essentials, in conformity with the "idealist" prescription whereby the surest way of healing the patient is to kill him; in our day, having failed to raise human society to the level of the religious ideal, one lowers religion to a level which is humanly accessible and rationally realizable, but which is nothing from the point of view of our integral intelligence and our possibilities of immortality. The exclusively human, far from being able to keep itself in equilibrium, always ends in the infra-human.

*　　　*　　　*

[5] It might seem that the spiritual decadence of the Romans must have been prejudicial to an imperial mission, but this is not so since the Romans possessed those qualities of strength and generosity—or tolerance—which are necessary for this providential function. Rome persecuted the Christians because they threatened everything which, in the eyes of the ancients, made Rome what it was; if Diocletian could have foreseen the edict of Theodosius abolishing the Roman religion, he would still not have acted otherwise than he did.

For traditional worlds, to be situated in space and time is to be situated respectively in a cosmology and an eschatology; time has a meaning only through the perfection of an origin that is to be maintained and in view of a final disintegration that casts us almost without transition at the feet of God. If there are sometimes developments in time which may seem progressive when isolated from the whole—in the formulation of doctrine, for example, or especially in art, which needs time and experience to ripen—this is not because tradition can be regarded as having become different or better, but on the contrary because it seeks to remain wholly itself or "to become what it is"; in other words, it is because traditional humanity seeks to manifest or externalize on a certain plane something it carries within itself and is in danger of losing, a danger that increases as the cycle unfolds, the cycle inevitably ending in decline and Judgment. It is therefore our increasing weakness, and with it the risk of forgetfulness and betrayal, which more than anything obliges us to externalize or make explicit what at the beginning was included in an inward and implicit perfection; Saint Paul needed neither Thomism nor cathedrals, for all profundities and splendors were in himself and all around him in the sanctity of the early community. And this, far from supporting iconoclasts of all kinds, refutes them completely; more or less late epochs—the Middle Ages, for example—have an imperious need for externalizations and developments, just as water from a spring, if it is not to be lost on its way, needs a channel made by nature or the hand of man; and just as the channel does not transform the water and is not meant to do so—for no water is better than spring water—so the externalizations and developments of a spiritual patrimony are there not to change that patrimony, but to transmit it as fully and effectively as possible.

An ethnic genius may prefer to emphasize one aspect or another—with every right to do so and all the more freely inasmuch as every ethnic genius comes from Heaven—but its function cannot be to falsify the primordial intentions; on the contrary, the vocation of this genius consists in making those intentions as transparent as possible to the mentality the genius represents. On the one hand there is symbolism, which is as rigorous as the laws of nature and no less diverse, and on the other hand there is creative genius, which in itself is free as the wind, but which is nothing without the language of Truth and providential symbols and which is never hurried or arbitrary; this is why it is absurd to declare, as is so often done in our day, that the Gothic style, for example, expresses its "times" and that for Christians of "today" it constitutes an "anachronism", that to "follow the Gothic" is "plagiarism" or "pastiche", and that we must create a style that conforms to "our times", and so on. This is to ignore the fact that Gothic art is situated in space before becoming the retrospective incarnation of an epoch; in order to depart from the specifically Gothic idiom, the Renaissance should have begun by understanding it, and understanding it would have implied grasping its intrinsic nature and timeless character; and if the Renaissance had understood the Gothic, there would have been no reason to depart from it, for it goes without saying that the abandonment of an artistic language must have a motive other than incomprehension and lack of spirituality. A style expresses at once a spirituality and an ethnic genius, and these two factors cannot be improvised; a collectivity can pass from one formal language to another insofar as an ethnic predominance or a flowering of spirituality demands it, but it can in no case wish to change its style on the pretext of giving expression to a "period", hence to relativity, and therefore to the very thing that calls into question the value of absoluteness, which is the sufficient reason of every tradition. The predominance of Germanic influence, or the rise of the creative consciousness of Germanic peoples, together with a predominance of the emotional side of Christianity, spontaneously gave rise to the formal language that later came to be referred to as "Gothic"; the French who created the cathedral did so as Franks and not as Latins, though this in no way prevented them from manifesting their Latin quality on other planes, even within the framework of their Germanness, nor must it be forgotten that, spiritually speaking, like all Christians they were Semites and that it is this mixture—with the addition of a Celtic contribution—which produced the genius of the mediaeval West. Nothing in our time justifies the desire for a new style; if men have become "different", they have done so in an illegitimate manner and through the operation of negative factors, by way of a series of Promethean betrayals such as the Renaissance; the illegitimate and the anti-Christian obviously cannot produce a Christian style, nor can they make a positive contribution to such a style. It could be argued that our epoch is so important a fact that it is impossible to ignore it, in the sense that one is obliged to take unavoidable situations into account; this is true, but the only conclusion to be drawn from it is that we ought to return to the most sober and severe of mediaeval forms, the poorest in a certain sense, so as to conform to the spiritual distress of our epoch; we should leave our anti-religious "times" and reintegrate ourselves into a religious "space". An art that does not express the unchanging and does not want to be unchanging itself is not a sacred art; the builders of cathedrals did not wish to create a new style—had they wanted to they could not have done so—but they wished without any "research" to impart to the changelessness of the Romanesque a look that seemed to them more ample and sublime or more explicit; they wanted to crown and not abolish. Romanesque art is more static and more intellectual than Gothic art, and the Gothic is more dynamic and more emotional than the Romanesque; but each style expresses spontaneously and without Promethean affectations the changelessly Christian.[6]

*   *   *

In speaking about ancient or traditional peoples it is important not to confuse healthy and integral civilizations with the great paganisms—for the term is justified here—of the Mediterranean and the Near East, of which Pharaoh and Nebuchadnezzar have become the classic incarnations and conventional images. What strikes one first in these "petrified" traditions of the Biblical world is a cult of the massive and gigantic, as well as a cosmolatry often accompanied by bloody or orgiastic rites, not forgetting an excessive development of magic and the arts of divination; in civilizations of this kind the supernatural is replaced by the magical, and the here-below is divinized while nothing is offered for the hereafter—at least in the exoterism, which in fact overwhelms everything else; a sort of

---

[6] The so-called "avant-garde" architecture of our epoch lays claim to being "functional", but it is so only in part and in a wholly exterior and superficial way, since it ignores functions that are not material or practical; it excludes two elements essential to human art, namely symbolism, which is as strict as truth, and a joy at once contemplative and creative, which is as gratuitous as grace. A purely utilitarian "functionalism" is perfectly inhuman in both its premises and its results, for man is not an exclusively greedy and cunning creature: he is not meant to be comfortable inside the mechanism of a clock; so true is this that functionalism itself feels the need to dress itself up in new fantasies, which are most paradoxically justified by the shameless assertion that they are part of the "style".

7

marmoreal divinization of the human is combined with a passionate humanization of the divine; potentates are demigods, and the gods preside over all the passions.[7]

A question that might arise here is the following: why did these old religions deviate into paganism and then become extinct, whereas a similar destiny seems to be excluded in the case of the great traditions that are alive today in both the West and the East? The answer is that traditions having a prehistoric origin are, symbolically speaking, made for "space" and not for "time"; that is, they saw the light in a primordial epoch when time was still but a rhythm in a spatial and static beatitude and when space or simultaneity still predominated over the experience of duration and change; historical traditions on the contrary must take the experience of "time" into account and must foresee instability and decadence, since they were born at periods when time had become like a fast-flowing and ever more devouring river and when the spiritual outlook had to be centered on the end of the world. The position of Hinduism is intermediate in the sense that it has a capacity, exceptional in a tradition of the primordial type, for rejuvenation and adaptation; it is thus at once prehistoric and historic and realizes in its own way the miracle of a synthesis between the gods of Egypt and the God of Israel.

But to return to the Babylonians: the stonelike character of this type of civilization cannot be explained solely by a tendency to excess; it is also explained by a sense of the immutable, as if one had seen primordial beatitude beginning to vanish and had therefore wished to build a fortress to stand against time, or as if one had sought to transform the whole tradition into a fortress, with the result that the spirit was stifled instead of being protected; seen from this angle the marmoreal and inhuman side of these paganisms looks like a titanic reaction of space against time. In this perspective the implacability of the stars is paradoxically combined with the passion of bodies;

[7] The cases of Greece and Egypt were much less unfavorable than those of post-Sumerian Mesopotamia or Canaan; the Greeks, like the Egyptians, possessed a complete eschatology and a relatively influential esoterism. The Biblical Pharaoh seems to represent an isolated case rather than a type; according to Clement of Alexandria, Plato owed much to the sages of Egypt. The least unfavorable case among the pre-monotheistic civilizations of the Near East was doubtless that of Persia, whose ancient tradition still survives today in India in the form of Parseeism. Muslims have a special respect for Cyrus as well as for Alexander the Great, and they venerate the wife of Pharaoh as a saint.

the stellar vault is always present, divine and crushing, whereas an overflowing life serves as a terrestrial divinity. From another point of view, many of the characteristics of the civilizations of antiquity are explained by the fact that in the beginning the celestial Law was of an adamantine hardness while at the same time life still retained something of the celestial; Babylon lived falsely on this sort of recollection, and yet at the very heart of the cruelest paganisms there were mitigations that can be accounted for by changes in the cyclical atmosphere. The celestial Law becomes less demanding as we approach the end of our cycle; Clemency increases as man becomes weaker. Christ's acquittal of the adulterous woman has this significance—apart from other equally possible meanings—as does the intervention of the angel in the sacrifice of Abraham.

*   *   *

No one would think of complaining about the mitigation of moral laws, and yet it is nonetheless proper to consider it, not in isolation but in its context, for it is the context that reveals its intention, its scope, and its value. In reality the mitigation of moral laws—to the extent it is not illusory—can represent an intrinsic superiority only on two conditions: first, that it confers a concrete advantage on society; and second, that it is not obtained at the cost of what gives meaning to life; respect for the human person must not open the door to a dictatorship of error and baseness, to the crushing of quality by quantity, to general corruption and the loss of cultural values, for if it does so it is, in relation to the ancient tyrannies, merely an opposite extreme and not the norm. When humanitarianism is no more than the expression of an over-valuation of the human at the expense of what is divine or the crude fact at the expense of truth, it cannot possibly be counted as a positive acquisition; it is easy to criticize the "fanaticism" of our ancestors when one has lost the very notion of saving truth, or to be "tolerant" when one derides religion.

Whatever the morality of the Babylonians[8] may have been, it must not be forgotten that certain kinds of behavior depend largely

[8] Their name is used here as a symbol because of the associations of ideas evoked by the very word "Babylon", and not in order to make out that they were necessarily the worst of all men or the only bad ones.

on circumstances and that collective man always remains a sort of wild animal, at least in the "Iron Age": the conquerors of Peru and Mexico were no better than Nebuchadnezzar, Cambyses, or Antiochus Epiphanus, and one could find analogous examples in the most recent history. Religions can reform the individual man with his consent—and it is never the function of religion to make up for the absence of this consent—but no one can bring about a fundamental change in that "thousand-headed hydra" which is collective man, and this is why nothing of the kind has ever been the aim of any religion; all that a revealed Law can do is curb the egoism and ferocity of society by channeling its tendencies more or less effectively. The goal of religion is to transmit to man a symbolic, yet adequate, image of the reality that concerns him, according to his real needs and ultimate interests, and to provide him with the means of surpassing himself and realizing his highest destiny; this destiny can never be of this world, given the nature of our spirit. The secondary goal of religion—with a view to the principal goal—is to make possible a sufficient equilibrium in the life of the collectivity or to safeguard within the framework of the natural malice of men a maximum of spiritual opportunities; if society must be protected against the individual, the individual for his part must be protected against society. There is endless talk about "human dignity", but it is rather too often forgotten that "*noblesse oblige*"; dignity is invoked in a world that is doing everything to empty it of its content and thus to abolish it. In the name of an indeterminate and unconditional "human dignity", unlimited rights are conceded to the basest of men, including the right to destroy everything that goes to make our real dignity, that is to say, everything on every plane that attaches us in one way or another to the Absolute. Of course truth obliges us to condemn the excesses of the aristocracy, but we can see no reason at all why it should not also confer a right to judge contrary excesses.

*   *   *

In those ancient times so much decried in our days, the rigors of earthly existence, including the wickedness of men, were on the whole accepted as an inexorable fatality, and their abolition was with good reason believed to be impossible; in the midst of the trials of life, those of the hereafter were not forgotten, and it was admitted moreover that man needs suffering as well as pleasure here below and that a collectivity cannot maintain itself in the fear of God and in piety by contact with nothing but the agreeable;[9] such was the thinking of the elite at all levels of society. Miseries, whose deep-seated cause is always the violation of a celestial norm as well as indifference toward Heaven and our final ends, are there to restrain the greedy illusions of men, rather in the same way as the carnivores are there to prevent the herbivores from degenerating or multiplying to excess, all this by virtue of universal equilibrium and the homogeneity of the world; to be aware of this is part of the fear of God. In light of this elementary wisdom, a progress conditioned by spiritual indifference and an idolatry of well-being taken as an end in itself cannot constitute a real advantage, that is, an advantage proportioned to our total nature and our immortal kernel; this is evident enough, but even in the most "believing" environments, people go so far as to claim that technical progress is an indisputable good and that it is thus a blessing even from the point of view of faith. In reality modern civilization gives in order to take: it gives the world but takes away God; and it is this that compromises even its gift of the world.[10]

In our day there is a stronger tendency than ever to reduce happiness to the level of economic well-being—which is moreover insatiable in the face of an indefinite creation of artificial needs and a base mystique of envy—but what is completely lost sight of when

---

[9] In speaking of society Mencius did not hesitate to say, "Grief and trouble bring life, whereas prosperity and pleasure bring death." This is the quasi-biological law of rhythms or the law of the pruning of trees and bushes expressed in lapidary terms. This was also the great argument of the American Indians when faced with the temptations and constraints of white civilization.

[10] Let us recall this passage, curiously overlooked in our times, from the New Testament: "Love not the world, neither the things that are in the world. If any man love the world, the love of the Father is not in him" (1 John 2:15). Saint Francis of Sales addresses the human soul in these words: "God did not put you in this world for any need He had of you, who are wholly useless to Him, but only in order to exercise in you His goodness, giving you His grace and His glory. For this He gave you the understanding to know Him, the memory to remember Him. . . . Since you have been created and put in the world with this intention, all actions contrary to this must be rejected and avoided, and those which serve for nothing to this end must be scorned, as vain and superfluous. Consider the misfortune of the world which never thinks of this, but lives as though it believed it was only created to build houses, plant trees, amass riches, and indulge in idle talk" (*Introduction à la vie dévote*, Ch. 10).

this outlook is projected into the past is that a traditional craft and a contact with nature and natural things are factors essential to human happiness. Now these are just the factors that disappear in industry, which demands all too often, if not always, an inhuman environment and "quasi-abstract" manipulations, gestures with no intelligibility and no soul, all in an atmosphere of frigid cunning; we have arrived beyond all possibility of argument at the antipodes of what the Gospel means when it enjoins us to "become as little children" and to "take no thought for the morrow". The machine transposes the need for happiness onto a purely quantitative plane, having no relation to the spiritual quality of work; it takes away from the world its homogeneity and transparency and cuts men off from the meaning of life. More and more we attempt to reduce our intelligence to what the machine demands and our capacity for happiness to what it offers; since we cannot humanize the machine, we are obliged, by a certain logic at least, to mechanize man; having lost contact with the human, we stipulate what man is and what happiness is.

A barren argument, some will say; this gives us the opportunity, at the risk of becoming involved in one more digression, to denounce a misuse of language or thought which is encountered almost everywhere and which is quite typical of contemporary "dynamism". An argument is not "barren" or "fruitful"; it is true or false. If it is true, it is all it should be, and it could not then in any case be "barren" in itself; if it is false, the question of its possible "fruitfulness" does not arise, for error cannot be otherwise than harmful or indifferent, according to the domains and proportions involved. One must react against this tiresome tendency to substitute a utilitarian and subjective choice—or a moral choice—for an intellectual and hence objective alternative and to put the "constructive" in place of the true, as if truth were not positive by its nature and as if anything useful could be done without it.[11]

An analogous misuse is commonly made of the notion of "charity"; according to a new orientation, it seems that Catholics should "understand" their opponents out of "charity" instead of

---

[11] A truth can be inopportune in regard to circumstances or in regard to the insufficiency of a particular subject or category of subjects, or it can be situated at an insignificant level and have no impact; but it goes without saying that what we have in view here are normal possibilities and logical relationships.

judging them with "egoism" and regarding them as adversaries; here again there is a confusion between totally unrelated domains. In reality the situation is very simple: faced by a common danger, oppositions among those who are threatened by it are in practice diminished; to say that the danger is common means that the opposition between the aggressor and the victims is eminently greater than the oppositions dividing the victims from one another; but in the absence of an aggressor or his threat, the original oppositions retain all their virulence or at least their urgency. In other words an "outward" opposition becomes "inward" for the opponents in relation to a third opponent who sets himself against what they hold in common; this is a logical or "physical" fact, free from any sentimentality. From a certain point of view the contradiction between Catholicism and Protestantism is essential and irreducible; from another point of view Catholics and Protestants believe in God, in Christ, and in the future life; now to say that Protestants are in no way adversaries of Catholics, or conversely, is just as illogical as to pretend they have no ideas or interests in common. For centuries practically the only denominational antagonism at the heart of Western Europe was the one produced by the Reformation, Protestantism being opposed from its birth and by definition to the ideas and interests of the Roman Church; they were what is called "enemies", even when no animosity between individuals is presumed[12] and however displeased the partisans of the new "charity" may be; but in our day the situation has changed, and rather abruptly, in the sense that the common interests and ideas of all Christians—and even of all religious believers, whoever they might be—find themselves threatened by a new power, a materialistic and atheistic scientism, whether of the "left" or the "right". It is evident that in such circumstances not only does what unites prevail in certain respects over what divides, but also that the dangers one denomination represents for another—or one religion for another[13]—become

[12] As for the unbelievers, they were not sufficiently dangerous to the Protestants, or even to the Catholics, to be the cause of a sentimental reconciliation between the two denominations.

[13] It is thus with good logic that Pius XII was able to say that the crusades were "family quarrels". If the Muslim menace was not a factor of union for Christians divided by schisms and heresies, it is because the menace was external and not internal as is the case with scientism: under Arab or Turkish domination, Christians

less or disappear; to lay claim all at once, and loudly, to a "charity" the Church is alleged to have lost sight of for a thousand years or more and to contrast it with the "narrowness" or the "egoism" of a "past age" is a very bad joke on the part of Catholics; in any case it is unconscious hypocrisy, like other sentimentalities of the same order, all the more because this so-called "charity" is fostered by a certain scorn of theology and a desire to dull or "neutralize" every doctrinal, hence intellectual, element. In the past an agreement was an agreement, and a disagreement was a disagreement; but in our day one pretends to "love" all that one is unable to suppress, and one feigns to believe that our fathers were neither intelligent enough nor charitable enough to be able to distinguish between ideas and men nor capable of loving immortal souls independently of the errors that affect them. To the objection that the masses were and are incapable of grasping these subtleties, we would say that the same applies the other way round: if too many subtleties are thrust upon them the result will be confusion of ideas and indifference; the average man is so made, as is easy to see. Be that as it may, to preach to a denominational adversary is to try to save his soul, hence to love him in a certain way; and to fight an adversary is to protect the saving message of God. Our times, so concerned with "understanding" and "charity"—though these words too often serve to mask unintelligence, complacency, calculation—excel beyond all question in not understanding, and in not wanting to understand, what the men of earlier times thought and did, men who were in many cases a hundred times better than their detractors.

But let us return after these digressions to matters that are more retrospective and in some respects less "up to date".

*   *   *

The knight of former days was faced finally with this sole alternative: the risk of death or the renunciation of the world; the greatness of the responsibility, the hazard, or the sacrifice coincides with the quality of "nobility"; to live nobly is to live in company with death,

---

remained Christians, whereas scientism empties the churches even in Christian countries. In the nineteenth century, the first lay government of a liberated Greece could find nothing better to do than to close several hundred convents, which had been untouched by the Muslims.

whether physical or spiritual. The knight had no right to lose sight of the fissures in existence; obliged to view things from an eminence, he could never be far from their nothingness. Furthermore, if one is to be able to rule others, one must know how to rule oneself; inward discipline is the essential qualification for the functions of chief, judge, or warrior. True nobility, which cannot in any case be the monopoly of an office, implies a penetrating consciousness of the nature of things and at the same time a generous giving of oneself, thus excluding idle fancies no less than baseness.[14]

The courts of princes must reflect the quality of a center, a hub, a summit, but they should not degenerate—as happened all too often—into a false paradise; the shimmering dream of Versailles was already a betrayal, fireworks without purpose and without greatness. Courts are normally centers for science, art, and magnificence; it is evident that they must not exclude austerity of habits—quite the contrary—for asceticism is not opposed to elegance any more than virtue is opposed to beauty, or conversely. Royal splendor and ceremonies are legitimate—or tolerable—by virtue of their spiritual symbolism and their political and cultural radiation and by virtue of the "divine right" of Caesar; the pageantry of the court is the "liturgy" of an authority conferred by the "mandate of Heaven"; but all that is nothing—let it be repeated once more—if the princes, or the nobles generally, do not in all respects teach by their example, beginning with the fear of God, without which no one has the right to demand respect and obedience. This is one of the principal functions of those who hold authority and power; the fact that in too many cases they have not been faithful to this function is what has brought about their fall; having forgotten Heaven, they have been forgotten by it.

But there is still something more to be said: all manifestations of princely splendor, whatever their symbolism and artistic value—and whether they are necessary or not—always carry within themselves the metaphysical seeds of their own ruin. Strictly speaking, only the

[14] Nothing is more false than the conventional opposition between "idealism" and "realism", which amounts to insinuating that the "ideal" is not "real", and conversely, as if an ideal situated outside reality had the smallest value and as if reality were always situated on a lower level than what may be called an "ideal"; to believe this is to think in a quantitative, not a qualitative, mode. We have in mind here the current meaning of the terms and not their specifically philosophical significance.

hermit is absolutely legitimate, for man was created alone and dies alone; we mention the hermit because he represents a principle and is therefore a symbol, but without confusing an outward isolation with holy solitude, which for its part can and must find a place in all human situations. Social virtues are nothing without this solitude and by themselves engender nothing lasting, for before acting one must be; it is this quality of being that is so sorely lacking in people today. It is forgetfulness of our solitude in God—of this terrestrial communion with celestial dimensions—which brings in its wake all human failings as well as all earthly calamities.

We could also express ourselves in the following way: in a traditional climate men live as if they are suspended from an ideal and invisible prototype, with which they are seeking to be reunited as their particular situations permit and according to their sincerity and vocation. Now every man should be a contemplative and live among men like a hermit as far as vocation is concerned; "worldliness" is an anomaly, strictly speaking; it has become illusorily normal only on account of the fall—or the successive falls—of man or a particular group of men. We are made for the Absolute, which embraces all things and from which none can escape, and this is marvelously expressed by the monotheistic alternative between the two "eternities" beyond the grave; whatever the metaphysical limitation of this concept, it nonetheless provokes in the soul of the believer an adequate presentiment of what the human condition is beyond the terrestrial matrix and in the face of the Infinite. The alternative may be insufficient from the point of view of total Truth, but it is psychologically realistic and mystically efficacious; many lives are squandered and lost for the single reason that a belief in hell and Paradise is lacking.

The monk or hermit—and every contemplative, even a king— lives as if in an antechamber of Heaven;[15] on this very earth and within his mortal body he has attached himself to Heaven and enclosed himself in a prolongation of those crystallizations of Light which are the celestial states. This being so, one understands how monks or nuns can see in the monastic life their "Paradise

---

[15] It is in an analogous sense, but one superior as to the degree of existence, that the Paradise *Sukhâvatî* is represented as surrounded by a golden thread; it is as if it were suspended from *Nirvâna*, and it is thus a joyful prison, which is cut off from suffering and is open only toward total Freedom.

on earth"; all things considered, they are at rest in the divine Will and wait for nothing in this world below except death, and in this way they have already passed through death; they live here below in keeping with Eternity. The days as they succeed one another do nothing but repeat the same day of God; time stops in a unique and blessed day and is thus joined once again to the Origin, which is also the Center. And it is this Elysian simultaneity that the ancient worlds have always had in view, at least in principle and in their nostalgia; a civilization is a "mystical body": as far as possible it is a collective contemplative.

*   *   *

These considerations lead us to the crucial problem of obedience, so essential in normal civilizations and so little understood in modern ones, which nevertheless have no trouble admitting it when it is a question of collective discipline, though it is sometimes to the detriment of the most elementary spiritual rights. Obedience in itself is a means of inward perfection, on condition that it is wholly supported by religion, as is the case in all traditional worlds: within this framework, a man must in any case obey someone or something, if only the sacred Law and his own conscience if he is a prince or pontiff; nothing and no one is independent of God. The subordination of women, children, inferiors, and servants falls into place quite normally in the system of multiple obediences that makes up a religious society; dependence with respect to another may be a hard fate, but it always has a religious meaning, as does poverty, which—no less than dependence—includes a similar significance in its very nature. From the point of view of religion, the rich and the independent are by no means by definition the happy ones; ease and freedom may indeed be elements of happiness in such a society, but from the point of view of religion they are so only in connection with piety and as a result of it, which brings us back to the adage that "*noblesse oblige*"; when piety exists apart from material well-being and impiety is on the contrary allied to it, true happiness is attributed to pious poverty, not impious wealth; and it is pure calumny to claim that religion as such, or through its institutions, has always been on the side of the rich. On the one hand religion is there to transform those human beings who are willing to allow themselves to be transformed, but on the other hand religion must take men as they are, with all their natural rights and their collectively ineradicable faults, or else it cannot survive in the world of men.

In the same line of thought, one more observation must be made, whether agreeable or not: a society as such, or by virtue of the mere fact of its existence, represents nothing of value; this implies that social virtues are nothing in themselves and apart from the spiritual context that orients them toward our final goal; to say otherwise is to falsify the very definition of man and of the human. The supreme Law is the perfect love of God—a love that must engage our whole being, as the Scripture says—and the second Law, that concerning love of the neighbor, is "like unto" the first; now "like unto" does not mean "equivalent to", and still less "superior to", but "of the same spirit"; Christ means that the love of God manifests itself extrinsically by love of the neighbor, wherever there is a neighbor, which is to say that we cannot love God while hating our fellow men. In conformity with our full human nature, love of the neighbor is nothing without love of God, from which it draws all its content and without which it has no meaning; of course loving the creature is also a way of loving the Creator, but on the express condition that its foundation is the direct love of God, for otherwise the second Law would not be the second but the first; now it is not said that the first law is "like unto" or "equal to" the second, but that the second is "like unto" the first, which means that the love of God is the necessary foundation and *conditio sine qua non* of all other charity. This relationship shines through—sometimes imperfectly but always recognizably with respect to its principle—in all traditional civilizations.

No world is perfect, but every human world should possess the means to perfection. A world has value and legitimacy because of what it does for the love of God and for nothing else; and by "love of God" we mean above all the choice of Truth and then the direction of the will: the Truth that makes us conscious of an absolute and transcendent Reality—at once personal and supra-personal—and the will that attaches itself to it and recognizes in it its own supernatural essence and final end.

Fall and Forfeiture

In antiquity and the Middle Ages man was "objective" in the sense
that his attitude was still largely determined by the element "object",[1]
on the plane of ideas as well as on that of the senses; he was very
far from the relativism of modern man, who compromises objective reality by reducing it to natural accidents lacking any higher
significance and symbolic quality, and also from a "psychologism",
which calls into question the value of the knowing subject and in
effect destroys the very idea of intelligence. To speak of the element
"object" on the plane of ideas is not a contradiction, for a concept,
while it is evidently a subjective phenomenon insofar as it is a
mental phenomenon, is at the same time—like every sensory phenomenon—an objective element for the subject that is aware of it;
truth comes in a sense from outside, presenting itself to the subject
who may or may not accept it. Held fast as it were to the objects of
his knowledge or his faith, ancient man was little disposed to grant
a determining role to psychological contingencies; his inner reactions, whatever their intensity, were determined by an object and
thereby had in his consciousness what could be termed an objective
cast. The object as such—the object considered in connection with
its objectivity—was the real, the basis, the immutable thing, and in
grasping the object one possessed the subject, the one being guar-
anteed by the other; of course this is always so for many men and in
certain respects even for every sane man, but our aim here—at the
risk of seeming to propound truisms—is to characterize positions
the outlines of which can be only approximate and the nature of
which is unavoidably complex. Be that as it may, to listen compla-
cently to the subject is to betray the object, which is to say that the
men of old would have had the impression of denaturing or losing
the object in paying too much attention to the subjective pole of
consciousness. It was only from the time of the Renaissance that the
European became "reflexive", hence subjective in a certain way; it

[1] In current usage, the words "objective" and "objectivity" often carry the meaning
of impartiality, but it is clearly not this derivative and secondary sense that we have
in view here.

is true that this reflexivity can in its turn have a perfectly objective quality, just as an idea received from without can have a subjective character because of some bias of interest or feeling in the subject, but this is not what we are speaking of here; what we are saying is that the man of the Renaissance began to analyze mental reflections and psychic reactions and thus became interested in the "subject" pole to the detriment of the "object" pole; in becoming "subjective" in this sense, he ceased to be symbolist and became rationalist, for reason is the thinking ego. This is what explains the psychological and descriptive tendency of the great Spanish mystics, a tendency that has been wrongly taken as evidence of superiority and as a kind of norm.

This transition from objectivism to subjectivism reflects and renews in its own way the fall of Adam and the loss of Paradise: in losing a symbolist and contemplative perspective, founded both on impersonal intelligence and on the metaphysical transparency of things, man has gained the fallacious riches of the ego; the world of divine images has become a world of words. In all cases of this kind, Heaven—or a heaven—is shut off from above us without our noticing the fact, and we discover in compensation an earth long unappreciated, or so it seems, a homeland that opens its arms to welcome its children and wants to make us forget all lost Paradises; it is the embrace of *Mâyâ*, the sirens' song; *Mâyâ*, instead of guiding us, imprisons us. The Renaissance thought it had discovered man, whose pathetic convulsions it admired; for secularism in all its forms, man as such had become good to all intents and purposes, and by the same token the earth had become good and looked immensely rich and unexplored; instead of living only "by halves" one could at last live fully, be fully man and fully on earth; one was no longer a kind of half-angel, fallen and exiled; one had become a whole being, but by the downward path. The Reformation, whatever certain of its intuitions may have been, had as an overall result the relegation of God to Heaven—a Heaven henceforth distant and more and more neutralized—on the pretext that God keeps close to us "through Christ" in a sort of Biblical atmosphere and that He resembles us as we resemble Him; such an atmosphere brought with it a quasi-miraculous enrichment of the aspect "subject" and "earth", but a prodigious impoverishment of the aspect "object" and "Heaven". For the Revolution,* the earth had become definitively and exclusively the goal of man; the "Supreme Being" was merely a ridiculed nostrum; the seemingly infinite multitude of things on earth called for an infinity of activities, which furnished a pretext against contemplation, that is, against repose in "being", in the profound nature of things; man was at last free to busy himself on the hither side of all transcendence with the discovery of the terrestrial world and the exploitation of its riches; there were no longer any symbols, any metaphysical transparency; there was no longer anything but the agreeable or disagreeable, the useful or useless, whence the anarchic and irresponsible development of the experimental sciences. The flowering of a dazzling "culture", which took place in or immediately after these epochs thanks to the appearance of numerous men of genius, seems clearly to confirm the deceptive impression of a liberation and a progress, indeed of a "great period", whereas in reality this development represents no more than a compensation on a lower plane such as cannot fail to occur when a higher plane is forsaken.

Once Heaven was closed and man in effect installed in God's place, the objective measures of things were lost, virtually or actually; they have been replaced by subjective measures, purely human and conjectural pseudo-measures, and thus man has become involved in a movement that cannot be halted, since in the absence of celestial and stable measures there is no longer any reason for it to be halted, so that in the end a stage is reached at which human measures are replaced by infra-human measures until the very idea of truth is abolished. The mitigating circumstances in such cases—for they are always present, at least for some individuals—consist in the fact that on the verge of every new fall, the order then existing shows a maximum of abuse and corruption, so that the temptation to prefer an apparently clean error to an outwardly soiled truth is particularly strong; in traditional civilizations, the mundane element does all it can to compromise in the eyes of the majority the principles governing that civilization, the majority itself being only too prone to worldliness, not of an aristocratic and lively type, but one that is ponderous and pedantic; it is not the people who are

---

* Translator's note: The reference is to the French Revolution of the late eighteenth century.

the victims of theocracy, but on the contrary theocracy that is the victim first of worldly aristocrats and then of the masses, who begin by being seduced and end in revolt.[2] What is sometimes called the "tendency of history" is only the law of gravity.

To state that the measures of ancient man were celestial and static amounts to saying that this man still lived "in space": time was merely the contingency which corroded all things and in the face of which values that are so to speak "spatial"—that is, permanent because definitive—had always to assert themselves anew. Space symbolizes origin and immutability; time is decadence, which carries us away from the origin while at the same time leading us toward the Messiah, the great Liberator, and toward the meeting with God. In rejecting or losing celestial measures, man has become the victim of time: in inventing machines that devour duration, man has torn himself away from the peacefulness of space and thrown himself into a whirlpool, from which there is no escape.

The mentality of today seeks in fact to reduce everything to temporal categories: a work of art, a thought, a truth have no value in themselves and independently of any historical classification, but only as a result of the time in which they are rightly or wrongly placed; everything is considered the expression of a "period", not

[2] The European monarchs of the nineteenth century made almost desperate efforts to dam the mounting tide of democracy, of which they had already—partially and despite themselves—become representatives, efforts that were vain in the absence of the one counterweight which alone could have re-established stability and which is none other than religion, sole source of the legitimacy and power of princes. They fought to maintain an order that was in principle religious, but they represented this order in forms that disavowed it; the very apparel of kings and all the other forms among which they lived proclaimed doubt, spiritual "neutralism", a dimming of faith, a bourgeois and down-to-earth worldliness. This was already true to a lesser degree in the eighteenth century, when the arts of dress, architecture, and craftsmanship expressed, if not democratic tendencies, at least a worldliness lacking in greatness and strangely insipid; in this incredible age all men had the air of lackeys—the nobles all the more since they were nobles—and a rain of rice-powder seemed to have fallen upon a world of dreams; in this half-amiable and half-despicable universe of marionettes, the Revolution, which merely took advantage of the previous suicide of the religious outlook and of greatness, could not but break out; the world of wigs was much too unreal. Analogous remarks—suitably attenuated to conform to eminently different conditions—apply to the Renaissance and even to the end of the Middle Ages; the causes of a downward slide are always the same when seen in relation to absolute values.

of a timeless and intrinsic value, and this is entirely in conformity with modern relativism and with a psychologism or biologism that destroys essential values.[3] This philosophy derives a maximum of originality from what in effect is nothing but a hatred of God; but since it is impossible to abuse directly a God in whom one does not believe, one abuses Him indirectly through the laws of nature,[4] and one goes so far as to disparage the very form of man and his intelligence, the intelligence with which one thinks and abuses. But there is no escaping immanent Truth: "The more he blasphemes," says Meister Eckhart, "the more he praises God."

We have already mentioned the passage from objectivity to a reflexive subjectivity—a phenomenon pointed out by Maritain—while emphasizing the ambiguous character of this development. The fatal result of a "reflexivity" that has become hypertrophied is a verbal inflation that makes a person less and less sensitive to the objective value of conceptual formulations; people have grown accustomed to "classifying" everything without rhyme or reason in a long series of superficial and often imaginary categories, so much so that the most decisive—and intrinsically the most evident—truths

[3] In order to "situate" the doctrine of a Scholastic, for example, or even of a Prophet, a "psychoanalysis" is prepared—it is needless to emphasize the monstrous pride implicit in such an attitude—and with an entirely mechanical and perfectly unreal logic, the "influences" to which this doctrine has been subject are laid bare; in the course of this process there is no hesitation in attributing to saints all kinds of artificial and even fraudulent conduct, but it is obviously forgotten, with satanic inconsequentiality, to apply the same principle to oneself and to explain one's own—supposedly "objective"—position by psychoanalytical considerations; in short, sages are treated as sick men, and one takes oneself for a god. In the same line of thinking, it is shamelessly asserted that there are no primary ideas: that they are due only to prejudices of a grammatical order—hence to the stupidity of the sages who were duped by them—and that their only effect has been to sterilize "thought" for thousands of years, and so forth; it is a case of expressing a maximum of absurdity with a maximum of subtlety. For procuring a feeling of self-satisfaction, there is nothing like the conviction of having invented gunpowder or of having stood Christopher Columbus' egg on its point!

[4] A contemporary writer whose name does not come to mind has written that death is something "rather stupid", but this small impertinence is in any case a characteristic example of the mentality in question; the same outlook—or the same taste—gave rise to a remark, met with some time ago, that a certain person had perished in a "stupid accident". It is always nature, fate, the Will of God, objective reality that is pilloried; it is subjectivity that sets itself up as the measure of things, and what a subjectivity!

go unrecognized because they are conventionally relegated into the category of things "seen and done with", and moreover this is done without remembering that "seeing" is not necessarily synonymous with "understanding"; a name like that of Jakob Boehme, for example, means theosophy, so "let us move on". Such habits prevent one from distinguishing between the "lived vision" of the sage and the mental virtuosity of the profane "thinker"; everywhere one sees only "literature", and moreover literature of such and such a "period". But clearly truth is not a personal affair; trees flourish and the sun rises without anyone having to ask who has drawn them forth from silence and darkness, and birds sing without being given names.

In the Middle Ages there were still only two or three types of greatness: the saint and the hero as well as the sage, and then on a lesser scale and as it were by reflection the pontiff and prince; the "genius" and "artist", those glories of the secular universe, had not yet been born. Saints and heroes are like the appearance of stars on earth, reascending after their death to the firmament, their eternal home; they are almost pure symbols, spiritual signs only provisionally detached from the celestial iconostasis in which they have been enshrined since the creation of the world.

*   *   *

Modern science, as it plunges dizzily downwards toward an abyss into which it hurtles like a vehicle without brakes—its speed increasing in geometrical progression—is another example of the loss of "spatial" equilibrium that is characteristic of contemplative and still stable civilizations. We criticize this science—and we are certainly neither the first nor the only to do so—not insofar as it studies some fragmentary field within the limits of its competence, but insofar as it lays claim in principle to total knowledge and insofar as it ventures conclusions requiring a supra-sensible and properly intellective wisdom, the existence of which it rejects out of prejudice; in other words, the foundations of this science are false because, from the "subject" point of view, it replaces Intellect and Revelation by reason and experience—as if it were not contradictory to lay claim to totality on an empirical basis—and because, from the "object" point of view, it replaces Substance by matter alone while denying the universal Principle or reducing it to matter or some kind of pseudo-absolute deprived of all transcendence.

In all epochs and in all countries there have been revelations, religions, wisdoms; tradition is a part of mankind just as man is a part of tradition. Revelation is in one sense the infallible intellection of the total collectivity to the extent this collectivity has providentially become the receptacle of a manifestation of the universal Intellect; the source of this intellection is not of course the collectivity as such, but the universal or divine Intellect inasmuch as it adapts itself to the conditions prevailing in a particular intellectual or moral collectivity, whether an ethnic group or one determined by more or less distinctive mental conditions. To say that Revelation is "supernatural" does not mean that it is contrary to nature, for nature can be taken to represent by extension all that is possible on any given level of reality, but that it does not originate at the level to which—rightly or wrongly—the epithet "natural" is usually applied; this "natural" level is none other than that of physical causes, hence of sensory and psychic phenomena considered in relation to those causes.

If there are no grounds for finding fault with modern science to the extent it studies a domain within the limits of its competence—the precision and effectiveness of its results are proof of this—it is nonetheless necessary to add this important reservation: the principle, the range, and the development of a science or an art is a function of Revelation and of the requirements of spiritual life, without forgetting those of social equilibrium; it is absurd to claim unlimited rights for something in itself contingent, such as science or art. By refusing to admit any possibility of serious knowledge outside its own domain, modern science—as we have already said—claims exclusive and total knowledge while making itself out to be empirical and non-dogmatic, and this, it must be insisted, is a flagrant contradiction; to reject all "dogmatism" and "apriorism" is simply not to use the whole of one's intelligence.

Science is supposed to inform us not only about what is in space but also about what is in time; as for the first kind of knowledge, no one denies that Western science has accumulated an enormous quantity of observations, but as for the second kind, which ought to reveal to us what the abysses of duration hold, science is more ignorant than any Siberian shaman, who can at least refer to a mythology, hence to an adequate symbolism. There is of course a gap between the physical knowledge—necessarily restricted—of a primitive hunter and that of a modern physicist; but measured against the extent of knowable things, that gap is a mere millimeter.

Nevertheless, the very precision of modern science, or of certain of its branches, has become seriously threatened—and from quite an unforeseen direction—by the intrusion of psychoanalysis, even of "surrealism" and other forms of the irrational set up as systems, or of existentialism, which is indeed not so much irrational as unintelligent, strictly speaking;[5] the exclusively rational cannot fail to provoke such interferences at least at its vulnerable points, such as psychology or the psychological—or "psychologizing"—interpretation of phenomena that are by definition beyond its reach.

It is not surprising that a science arising out of the fall—or one of the falls—and out of an illusory rediscovery of the sensory world would also be a science of nothing but the sensory or what is virtually sensory,[6] that it would deny everything that transcends this domain, and that it would thus deny God, the hereafter, and the soul,[7] including *a fortiori* the pure Intellect, which is capable of knowing everything that modern science rejects, precisely; for the same reasons it also denies Revelation, which for its part rebuilds the bridge broken by the fall. According to the observations of experimental science, the blue sky that stretches above us is not a world of beatitude, but an optical illusion due to the refraction of light by the atmosphere, and from this point of view it is obviously right to deny that the home of the blessed can be found there; but it would be a great mistake to deny that the association of ideas between the visible heaven and celestial Paradise results from the nature of things and not from ignorance and naiveté mixed with imagination and sentimentality, for the blue sky is a direct and therefore adequate symbol of higher—and supra-sensory—degrees of Existence; it is even in fact a distant reverberation of those degrees, and it is necessarily so since it is truly a symbol, consecrated by the sacred

[5] That is, applying the intellectual norms that are indispensable here since it is a question of "philosophy".

[6] This distinction is necessary to meet the objection that science operates with elements inaccessible to our senses.

[7] We are not saying that all scientists deny these realities, but science denies them, and this is quite a different thing.

26

Scriptures and the unanimous intuition of peoples.[8] The nature of a symbol is intrinsically so concrete and so efficacious that celestial manifestations, when they occur in our sensory world, "descend" to earth and "reascend" to Heaven; sensory symbolism is a function of the supra-sensible reality it reflects. Light-years and the relativity of the space-time relationship have absolutely nothing to do with the symbolism—perfectly "exact" and "positive"—of appearances and its connection at once analogical and ontological with the celestial or angelic orders; the fact that the symbol itself may be no more than an optical illusion in no way impairs either its precision or efficacy, for all appearances, including those of space and the galaxies, are strictly speaking only illusions created by relativity.

One of the effects, among others, of modern science has been that of mortally wounding religion by posing in concrete terms problems which esoterism alone can resolve and which remain unresolved because esoterism is not heeded and is heeded less now than ever. Faced by these new problems, religion is disarmed, and it borrows clumsily and gropingly the arguments of the enemy, and this obliges it to falsify imperceptibly its own perspective and more and more to disavow itself; its doctrine is certainly not affected, but false opinions borrowed from its repudiators corrode it insidiously "from within", as witnessed by modernist exegesis, the demagogic leveling of the liturgy, Teilhardian Darwinism, "worker-priests", and a "sacred art" of surrealist and "abstract" persuasion. Scientific discoveries prove nothing to contradict the traditional positions of religion, of course, but there is no one at hand to point this out; too many "believers" assume on the contrary that it is up to religion to "shake off the dust of centuries", that is, to "liberate" itself from everything that makes up—or manifests—its essence; the absence of metaphysical or esoteric knowledge, on the one hand, and the suggestive force emanating from scientific discoveries as well as from collective psychoses, on the other, make religion an almost defenseless victim, a victim that in large measure refuses even to make use of the arguments at its disposal. It would nevertheless be easy, instead of slipping into the errors of others, to demonstrate that a world fabricated by scientism tends everywhere to turn ends

[8] To speak of a "symbol" is to speak of "participation" or "aspect", whatever the differences of level.

into means and means into ends and that it results either in a mystique of envy, bitterness, and hatred or in a fatuous materialism destructive of qualitative distinctions; that science, though neutral in itself—for facts are facts—is nonetheless a seed of corruption and annihilation in the hands of man, who on average does not have a sufficient knowledge of the profound nature of Existence to be able to integrate—and thereby neutralize—the facts of science within a total view of the world; that the philosophical consequences of science imply fundamental contradictions; and that man has never been so ill-known and so misinterpreted as from the moment he was subjected to the "x-rays" of a psychology founded on postulates that are radically false and contrary to his nature.

Modern science presents itself in the world as the principal or sole purveyor of truth; according to this style of certainty, to know Charlemagne is to know his brain-weight and how tall he was. From the standpoint of total truth—let it be said once more—it is a thousand times better to believe that God created the world in six days and that the hereafter lies beneath the flat surface of the earth or in the revolving heavens than it is to know the distance from one nebula to another while not knowing that phenomena merely serve to manifest a transcendent Reality which determines us in every respect and which gives to our human condition its whole meaning and content; thus the great traditions, aware that a Promethean knowledge must lead to the loss of the essential and saving truth, have never prescribed nor encouraged this accumulation of a knowledge that is completely outward and in fact mortal to man. It is currently asserted that such and such a scientific achievement "does honor to humanity", together with other foolishness of the same kind, as if man could do honor to his nature otherwise than by transcending himself and as if he could transcend himself otherwise than in consciousness of the absolute and in sanctity.

In the opinion of most of our contemporaries, experimental science is justified by its results, which are in fact dazzling from a certain fragmentary point of view; but one readily loses sight, not only of the fact that bad results definitively end up prevailing over good, but also of the spiritual devastation inherent in the scientific outlook *a priori* and by its very nature, a devastation for which its positive results—always outward and partial—can never compensate. In any case it savors of temerity in our day to dare recall the most forgotten of Christ's sayings: "For what shall it profit a man, if he shall gain the whole world, and lose his own soul?"

*   *   *

If the unbeliever rebels against the idea that all his actions will be weighed, that he will be judged and perhaps condemned by a God whom he cannot grasp, that he will have to expiate his faults and even simply his sin of indifference, it is because he lacks the sense of immanent equilibrium and that of the majesty of Existence, of the human state in particular. To exist is no small matter; the proof is that no one can extract from nothingness a single speck of dust; similarly, consciousness is not nothing; we cannot bestow the least spark of it on an inanimate object. The hiatus between nothingness and the least of objects is absolute, and in the last analysis this absoluteness is that of God.[9]

What is outrageous in those who assert that "God is dead" or even "buried"[10] is that in doing so they inevitably put themselves in place of what they deny: whether they want to or not, they fill the vacuum psychologically left by the loss of the notion of God, and this confers on them provisionally—and paradoxically—a false superiority and even a kind of pseudo-absoluteness, or a kind of false realism stamped with icy loftiness or if need be with false modesty. Thenceforth their existence—and that of the world—is terribly lonely when faced with the vacuum created by the "inexistent God";[11] it is the world and themselves—they who are the brains of the world!—who henceforth carry the whole weight of universal Being instead of having the possibility of resting in it, as is demanded by human nature and above all by truth. Their

[9] It should not be forgotten that God as Beyond-Being or supra-personal Self is absolute in an intrinsic sense, whereas Being or the divine Person is absolute extrinsically, that is, in relation to His manifestation or to creatures, but not as such nor with respect to the Intellect, which "penetrates the depths of God".

[10] There are Catholics who do not hesitate to hold such views about the Greek Fathers and the Scholastics, doubtless in order to compensate a certain "inferiority complex".

[11] In reality God is not "existent" either, meaning that He cannot be reduced to the level of the existence of things. In order to make it clear that this reservation implies no kind of privation, it would be better to say that God is "not-existent".

poor individual existence—not Existence as such insofar as they participate in it, which moreover appears to them "absurd" to the degree they have any idea of it at all[12]—is condemned to a kind of divinity or rather to a superficial semblance of divinity, whence the appearance of superiority we have already mentioned, a posed and polished ease readily combined with a charity steeped in bitterness and in reality set against God.

The artificial isolation in question accounts moreover for the mystique of "nothingness" and "anguish" as well as for the astonishing prescription of liberation by action and even "commitment" to action: deprived of divine "existentiation" or believing himself so to be, man must find something to take its place or else collapse into his own nothingness through an ersatz "existence", and this he does precisely by "committed" action.[13] But all this is at root only an imaginative and sentimental capitulation to the machine: since the machine has no value except by virtue of what it produces, man exists only by virtue of what he does and not because of what he is; now man defined by action is no longer man: he is a beaver or ant.

In the same line of thought, attention must be drawn to the need for false absolutes on all planes, whence the silly theatricality of modern artists; ancient man, who had a sense of the relativity of values and who put everything in its place, appears to be mediocre by comparison, "self-satisfied" and hypocritical. The mystical fervor that is a part of human nature is deflected from its normal objects and absurdly squandered; it is put into a still life or a play, when it is not applied to the trivialities that characterize the reign of the machine and the masses.

Independently of doctrinal atheism and cultural particularities, modern man moves through the world as if Existence were nothing or as if he had invented it; it is for him a commonplace thing like the dust beneath his feet—more especially as he is no longer aware

---

[12] This idea is reduced to the perception of the world and things and is therefore quite indirect.

[13] It is forgotten that the sages or philosophers who have determined intellectual life for hundreds or thousands of years—we are not speaking of Prophets—were in no way "committed to action", or rather that their "commitment" was in their work, which is fully sufficient; to think otherwise is to seek to reduce intelligence or contemplation to action, which is typical of existentialism.

of the Principle at once transcendent and immanent—and he makes use of it with assurance and inadvertence in a life that has lost its sacredness and thus become meaningless. Everything is conceived through a web of contingencies, relationships, prejudices; no phenomenon is any longer considered in itself, in its being, and grasped at its root; the contingent has usurped the rank of the absolute; man scarcely reasons any more except in terms of his imagination, which is falsified by ideologies on the one hand and by his artificial surroundings on the other. Now eschatological doctrines, however exaggerated they may appear to the sensibilities of those whose only gospel is their materialism and dissipation and whose life is nothing but a flight before God, provide the true measure for the cosmic situation of man; what the Revelations ask of us and what Heaven imposes or inflicts on us is what we are in reality, regardless of our own opinion; we know it in our heart of hearts, if only we can detach ourselves a little from the monstrous accumulation of false images that have become entrenched in our mind. What we need is to become once again capable of grasping the value of Existence and, amid the multitude of phenomena, the meaning of man; we must once again find the measure of the real. Our reactions to eschatological doctrines—or to the one that concerns us most—are the measure of our understanding of man.

There is something in man which is able to conceive the Absolute and even attain to it and which therefore is absolute. This being the case, one can assess the extent of the aberration of those for whom it seems perfectly natural to have the right or chance to be man, but who wish to be so without participating in the integral nature of man and the attitudes it implies. Needless to say, the paradoxical possibility of denying itself is also a part of this nature—for to be man is to be free in a "relatively absolute" sense—much in the same way as to accept error or throw oneself into an abyss is a human possibility.

We have already said that "unbelievers" no longer have the sense of either nothingness or existence, that they no longer know the value of existence and never look at it in relation to the nothingness from which it is miraculously detached. Miracles in the usual sense of the word are in effect only particular variants of the initial—and everywhere present—miracle that is the fact of existence; the miraculous and divine are everywhere; it is the human outlook that is absent.

Fundamentally there are only three miracles: existence, life, intelligence; with intelligence, the curve springing from God closes on itself like a ring that in reality has never been parted from the Infinite.

*   *   *

When the modern world is contrasted with traditional civilizations, it is not simply a question of looking on each side for what is good and bad; since good and evil are everywhere, it is essentially a question of knowing on which side the lesser evil is to be found. If someone tells us that such and such a good exists outside tradition, we respond: no doubt, but it is necessary to choose the most important good, and this is necessarily represented by tradition; and if someone tells us that in tradition there exists such and such an evil, we respond: no doubt, but it is necessary to choose the lesser evil, and again it is tradition that contains it. It is illogical to prefer an evil that involves some benefits to a good that involves some evils.

Certainly, to confine oneself to admiring the traditional worlds is still to stop short at a fragmentary point of view, for every civilization is a "two-edged sword"; it is a total good only by virtue of those invisible elements that determine it positively. In certain respects, every human society is bad; if its transcendent character is entirely removed—which amounts to dehumanizing it since the element of transcendence is essential to man though always dependent upon his free consent—then at the same time society's entire reason for being is removed, and there remains only an ant heap in no way superior to any other ant heap since the needs of life and thus the right to life remain everywhere the same, whether it is a question of men or insects. It is one of the most pernicious of errors to believe that the human collectivity, on the one hand, or its well-being, on the other, represents an unconditional or absolute value and thus an end in itself.

Regarded as social phenomena and independently of their intrinsic value—though there is no sharp dividing line between the two—traditional civilizations, despite their inevitable imperfections, are like sea walls built to stem the rising tide of worldliness, error, subversion, of the fall that is ceaselessly renewed; this fall is more and more invasive, but it will be conquered in its turn by the final irruption of divine fire, the very fire of which the traditions are, and always have been, the earthly crystallizations. To reject traditional frameworks because of human abuses amounts to asserting that the founders of religion did not know what they were doing, that abuses are not inherent in human nature, that they are therefore avoidable even in societies numbering millions of men, and that they are avoidable thanks to purely human means; no more flagrant contradiction than this could be imagined.

*   *   *

In a certain sense, the sin of Adam was a sin of curiosity. *A priori,* Adam saw contingencies in connection with their attachment to God and not as independent entities. Anything considered in this connection is beyond evil; now to desire to see contingency in itself is to desire to see evil and also to see the good to the extent it contrasts with evil. As a result of this sin of curiosity—Adam wanted to see the "other side" of contingency—Adam himself and the whole world fell into contingency as such; the link with the divine Source was broken and became invisible; the world suddenly became external to Adam: things became opaque and heavy and like unintelligible and hostile fragments. And this drama is always repeating itself anew, in collective history as well as in the life of individuals.

A meaningless knowledge—one to which we have no right either by virtue of its nature or our capacities or therefore by virtue of our vocation—is not a knowledge that enriches, but one that impoverishes. Adam had become poor after having acquired knowledge of contingency as such or contingency insofar as it limits.[14] We must distrust the fascination abysses can exert over us; it is in the nature of cosmic impasses to seduce and play the vampire; the current of forms does not want us to escape its hold. Forms can be snares just as they can be symbols and keys: beauty can chain us to forms just as it can be a door to the non-formal.

Or again, from a slightly different point of view: the sin of Adam consists basically in having wished to superimpose something on

[14] A *hadîth* says: "I seek refuge with God in the face of a science that is of no use to me"; and another: "It is one of the claims to nobility of a Muslim not to pay attention to what is not his concern." One must remain in primordial innocence and not seek to know the Universe in detail. This thirst for knowledge—as the Buddha said—confines man to *Samsâra.*

Existence, which was beatitude; Adam thereby lost this beatitude and was engulfed in the restless and disappointing turmoil of superfluous things.[15] Instead of reposing in the immutable purity of Existence, fallen man is drawn into the whirling dance of existing things, which as accidents are delusive and perishable. In the Christian cosmos, the Blessed Virgin is the incarnation of this snow-like purity; she is inviolable and merciful like Existence or Substance; God in assuming flesh brought with Him Existence, which is as it were His throne; He caused it to precede Him, and through it He came into the world. God can enter into the world only through virgin Existence.

*   *   *

The problem of the fall evokes the problem of that universal theophany which is the world. The fall is only one particular link in this process; moreover it is not everywhere presented as a "fault", but in certain myths takes the form of an event unconnected with human or angelic responsibility. If there is a cosmos, a universal manifestation, there must also be a fall or falls, for to say "manifestation" is to say "other than God" and "remotion".

On earth, the divine Sun is veiled; as a result the measures of things are relative, man can take himself for what he is not, and things can appear to be what they are not; but once the veil is torn, at the time of the birth we call death, the divine Sun appears; measures become absolute; beings and things become what they are and follow the ways of their true nature.

This does not mean that the divine measures do not reach our world, but they are as it were "filtered" by its existential shell, and from having been absolute they become relative, whence the fluctuating and indeterminate character of earthly things. The solar star is none other than Being seen through this shell; in our microcosm, the sun is represented by the heart.[16]

It is because we live in all respects in such a shell that we need—in order to know who we are and where we are going—that cosmic

---

[15] "Rivalry in worldly increase distracteth you" (*Sûrah* "Rivalry in Worldly Increase" [102]:1).

[16] And the moon is the brain, which is identified macrocosmically—if the sun is Being—with the central reflection of the Principle in manifestation, a reflection susceptible to "waxing and waning" in accordance with its contingent nature and

rending which is Revelation; and it could be pointed out in this connection that the Absolute never consents to become relative in a total and uninterrupted manner.

In the fall and its repercussions throughout duration, we see the element "absoluteness" finally devoured by the element "contingency"; it is in the nature of the sun to be devoured by the night just as it is in the nature of light to "shine in the darkness" and "not to be comprehended". Numerous myths express this cosmic fatality, inscribed in the very nature of what we may call the "reign of the demiurge".

The prototype of the fall is none other than the process of universal manifestation itself. To speak of manifestation, projection, "alienation", going forth is to speak also of regression, reintegration, return, *apocatastasis*; the error of the materialists—whatever subtleties they may employ in seeking to dissolve the conventional and now "obsolete" idea of matter—is to take matter as their starting point as if it were a primordial and stable fact, whereas it is only a movement, a sort of transitory contraction of a substance that is in itself inaccessible to our senses. Our empirical matter, with all it comprises, is derived from a supra-sensory and eminently plastic proto-matter; it is in this proto-matter that the primordial terrestrial being is reflected and "incarnated", which is expressed in Hinduism in the myth of the sacrifice of *Purusha*. Because of the tendency to segmentation inherent in this proto-matter, the divine image was broken and diversified; but creatures were still, not individuals who tear one another to pieces, but contemplative states derived from angelic models and, through them, from divine Names, and in this sense it could be said that in Paradise sheep lived side by side with lions; what are in question here are only the "hermaphroditic" prototypes—supra-sensorial and spherical in form—of divine possibilities, which stem from the qualities of "clemency" and "rigor",

---

therefore also with cyclic contingencies. These correspondences are of such a complexity—a single element can assume various meanings—that we can mention them only in passing. It is sufficient to add that the sun itself also represents—and necessarily so—the divine Spirit manifested and that on this account it must "wane" in setting and "wax" in rising; it gives light and heat because it is the Principle, and it sets because it is but the manifestation of the Principle. From this point of view, the moon is the peripheral reflection of this manifestation. Christ is the sun, and the Church is the moon; "It is expedient for you that I go away", but the "Son of man will come again".

"beauty" and "strength", "wisdom" and "joy". In this proto-material *hylê* occurred the creation of the species and of man, a creation resembling the "sudden crystallization of a supersaturated chemical solution";[17] after the "creation of Eve"—the bipolarization of the primordial "androgyne"—there occurred the "fall", namely, the "exteriorization" of the human couple, which brought in its train—since in the subtle and luminous proto-matter everything was bound together and interdependent—the exteriorization or "materialization" of all other earthly creatures, hence their "crystallization" in sensible, heavy, opaque, and mortal matter.

One recalls the tradition that the human body, or even simply any living body, is like half a sphere; all our faculties and movements look and tend toward a lost center—which we feel as if "in front" of us—lost, but found again symbolically and indirectly in sexual union. But the result is only a grievous renewal of the drama: a fresh entry of the spirit into matter. The opposite sex is only a symbol: the true center is hidden within ourselves, in the heart-intellect. The creature recognizes something of the lost center in his partner; the love that results from this is like a distant shadow of the love of God and the intrinsic beatitude of God; it is also a shadow of the knowledge which consumes forms as by fire and which unites and delivers.

The whole cosmogonic process is found again in static mode in man: we are made of matter, that is, of sensible density and "solidification", but at the center of our being is supra-sensible and transcendent Reality, at once infinitely fulgurant and infinitely peaceful. To believe that matter is the "alpha" from which everything began amounts to asserting that our body is the starting point of our soul, hence that the origin of our ego, our intelligence, and our thoughts is in our bones, our muscles, our organs; in reality, if God is the "omega", He is necessarily also the "alpha", on pain of absurdity. The cosmos is a "message from God to Himself by Himself", as the Sufis would say, and God is "the First and the Last", and not only the Last. There is a sort of "emanation", but it is strictly discontinuous because of the transcendence of the Principle and the essential incommensurability of the degrees of reality; emanationism on the

---

[17] An expression used by Guénon in speaking of the realization of "the supreme Identity". It is plausible to consider deification as resembling—in the opposite direction—its antipode, creation.

contrary postulates a continuity, which would affect the Principle as a result of manifestation. It has been said that the visible universe is an explosion and thus a dispersion starting from a mysterious center; what is certain is that the total Universe, the greater part of which is invisible to us in principle and not solely *de facto*, describes some such movement—symbolically speaking—and arrives finally at the end point of its expansion; this point is determined first by relativity in general and then by the initial possibility of the cycle in question. The living being itself resembles a crystallized explosion, if one may so express it; it is as if the being had been turned to crystal by dread before God.

*   *   *

Having shut himself off from access to Heaven and having several times repeated—within ever narrower limits—his initial fall, man has ended by losing his intuition of everything that transcends himself, and he has thereby sunk below his own nature, for one cannot be fully man except through God, and the earth is beautiful only through its link with Heaven. Even when a man still believes, he forgets more and more what religion really demands: he is astonished at the calamities of this world, without its occurring to him that they may be acts of grace since—like death—they rend the veil of earthly illusion and thus allow man "to die before dying", hence to conquer death.

Many people imagine that purgatory or hell are for those who have killed, stolen, lied, committed fornication, and so on and that it suffices to have abstained from these actions to merit Heaven; in reality the soul is consigned to the flames for not having loved God or for not having loved Him enough; this can be understood if we recall the supreme Law of the Bible: to love God with all our faculties and all our being. The absence of this love[18] does not necessarily involve murder or lying or some other transgression, but it does necessarily involve indifference;[19] and indifference, which is

---

[18] It is not exclusively a question of a *bhakti*, of an affective and sacrificial path, but simply of the fact of preferring God to the world, whatever the mode of this preference; "love" in the Scriptures thus also embraces the sapiential paths.

[19] Fénelon was right to see in indifference the gravest of the ills of the soul.

the most generally widespread of faults, is the very hallmark of the fall. It is possible for the indifferent[20] not to be criminals, but it is impossible for them to be saints; it is they who go in by the "wide gate" and follow the "broad way", and it is of them that Revelation says, "So then because thou art lukewarm, and neither cold nor hot, I will spew thee out of my mouth" (3:16). Indifference toward truth and toward God borders on pride and is not free from hypocrisy; its seeming harmlessness is full of complacency and arrogance; in this state of soul the individual is content with himself even if he accuses himself of minor faults and appears modest, which in fact commits him to nothing but on the contrary reinforces his illusion of being virtuous. It is this criterion of indifference that makes it possible for the "average man" to be so to speak "caught in the act", for the most surreptitious and insidious of vices to be as it were taken by the throat, and for every man to have his poverty and distress proven to him; in short it is indifference that is "original sin" or its most general manifestation.

Indifference is diametrically opposed to spiritual impassibility or contempt of vanities as well as to humility. True humility is to know that we can add nothing to God and that, even if we possessed all possible perfections and had accomplished the most extraordinary works, our disappearance would take nothing away from the Eternal.

Even believers themselves are for the most part too indifferent to feel concretely that God is not only "above" us "in Heaven", but also "ahead" of us, at the end of the world or even simply at the end of our life; that we are drawn through life by an inexorable force and that at the end of the course God awaits us; that the world will be submerged and swallowed up one day by an unimaginable irruption of the purely miraculous—unimaginable because surpassing all human experiences and standards of measurement. Man cannot possibly draw on his experience to bear witness to anything of the kind any more than a mayfly can expatiate on the alternation of the seasons; for a creature that is born at midnight and whose life will last but a day, the rising of the sun can in no way enter into the series of its habitual sensations; the sudden appearance of the solar disk, unforeseeable by reference to any analogous phenomenon

---

[20] The *ghâfilûn* of the Koran.

that had occurred during the long hours of darkness, would seem like an unheard of and apocalyptic prodigy. Now it is thus that God will come. There will be nothing but this one advent, this one presence, and by it the world of experiences will be shattered.

*   *   *

In man stamped by the fall, action not only has priority over contemplation, but even abolishes it; normally the alternative should not present itself, contemplation being in its essential nature neither allied to action nor opposed to it; but fallen man is precisely not "normal" man in the absolute sense. We could also say that in some respects there is harmony between contemplation and action whereas in other respects there is opposition; but any such opposition is extrinsic and quite accidental. There is harmony in the sense that in principle nothing can be opposed to contemplation—this is the initial thesis of the *Bhagavad Gîtâ*—and there is opposition to the extent their planes differ: just as it is impossible to contemplate a nearby object and at the same time the distant landscape behind it, so it is impossible—in this connection alone—to contemplate and act at the same time.[21]

Fallen man is man led on by action and imprisoned by it, and this is why he is also sinful man; the moral alternative arises less from action than from the exclusivism of action, that is, from individualism and its illusory "extra-territoriality" with regard to God; action becomes in a sense autonomous and totalitarian whereas

---

[21] This is what the tragedy of Hamlet expresses: there were facts and actions, and demands of action, but the Shakespearean hero, seeing through it all, saw only principles or ideas; he sank into things as into a morass; their very vanity or unreality prevented him from acting, dissolved his action; he had before him, not this or that evil, but evil as such, and the inconsistency, absurdity, and incomprehensibility of the world thwarted everything he wished to do. Contemplation either removes one from action by causing the objects of action to disappear, or it renders action perfect by making God appear in the agent; now the contemplativity of Hamlet had unmasked the world, but it was not yet fixed in God; it was as it were suspended between two planes of reality. In a certain sense, the drama of Hamlet is that of the *nox profunda*; it is also perhaps, in a more outward sense, the drama of the contemplative who is forced to action but has no vocation for it; it is in any case a drama of profundity faced with the unintelligibility of the human comedy.

it ought to fit into a divine context, a state of innocence in which there would be no separation of action from contemplation.

Fallen man is simultaneously squeezed and torn asunder by two pseudo-absolutes: the ponderous "I" and the dissipating "thing", the subject and the object, the ego and the world. As soon as he wakes up in the morning man remembers who he is, and immediately he thinks of one thing or another; between ego and object there is a link, which is usually action, whence a ternary encapsulated in the phrase: "I do this", or what amounts to the same thing: "I want this". Ego, act, and thing are in effect three idols, three screens hiding the Absolute; the sage is he who puts the Absolute in place of these three terms: it is God within him who is the transcendent and real Personality, hence the Principle of his "I";[22] his act is then the affirmation of God in the widest sense, and his object is again God;[23] this is what is realized in the most direct way possible by quintessential prayer—or concentration—which embraces virtually or effectively all of life and the entire world; in a more outward and more general sense, every man ought to see the three elements "subject", "act", and "object" within God to the extent he is capable through his gifts and through grace.

Fallen man is a fragmentary being, and therein lies for him a danger of deviation; for to speak of the fragmentary is, precisely, to speak of a lack of equilibrium. In Hindu terms, one would say that primordial man, *hamsa*, was still without caste; now the *brâhmana* does not correspond exactly to the *hamsa* but is only his uppermost fragment, or else he would by definition possess the full qualification of the warrior-king, the *kshatriya*, which is not the case; but every *Avatâra* is necessarily *hamsa*, and so is every *jîvan-mukta*, everyone "liberated in this life".

A parenthesis may be permissible at this point. We have often spoken about the "naturally supernatural" transcendence of the Intellect; now one must not lose sight of the fact that this transcendence can act without impediment only on condition of being framed by two supplementary elements, one human and the other divine, namely, virtue and grace. By "virtue" we do not mean the

[22] "Christ in me", as Saint Paul would say.
[23] This corresponds to the Sufic ternary "the invoker, the invocation, the Invoked" (*dhâkir, dhikr, Madhkûr*).

natural qualities that necessarily accompany a high degree of intellectuality and contemplativity, but a conscious and permanent effort
toward perfection, which is essentially effacement, generosity, and
love of truth; by "grace" we mean the divine aid which man must
implore and without which he can do nothing, whatever his gifts;
for a gift serves no purpose unless it is blessed by God.[24] The Intellect is infallible in itself, but the human receptacle is no less subject
to contingencies, which—though they cannot modify the intrinsic
nature of intelligence—can nonetheless oppose its full actualization
and the purity of its radiance.

That said, let us return to the problem of action. The process
and even the results of the fall are repeated on a reduced scale in
every outward or inward act that is contrary to universal harmony
or to a reflection of that harmony such as a sacred Law. The man
who has sinned has in the first place allowed himself to be seduced
and in the second place has ceased to be what he was before; he is
as it were branded by the sin, and he is so of necessity since every
act must bear its fruit; every sin is a fall and thereby "the fall". In
speaking of "sin" we mean to distinguish between a "relative" or
extrinsic sin, an "absolute"[25] or intrinsic sin, and then a sin of intention: a sin is "relative" which contravenes only a specific system of
morality—such as polygamy in the case of Christians or wine in
the case of Muslims—but which by the very fact of this contraven-
tion amounts in effect for those concerned to "absolute sin", as is
proven by the punishments in the hereafter decreed by the respec-
tive Revelations; nonetheless certain "relative sins" can become
legitimate—within the very framework of the Law that condemns
them—in special circumstances; this is the case, for example, with
murder in war. A sin is "absolute" or intrinsic which is contrary to
every code of morality and is excluded in all circumstances, such as
blasphemy or contempt for truth; as for a sin of intention, such as
hypocrisy, it is outwardly in conformity with a given moral code or
with all moral codes, but inwardly opposed to the divine Nature. We

[24] In certain disciplines it is the guru who acts on behalf of God; practically speaking
the result is the same if the conditions—and imponderables—of the spiritual climate in question are taken into account.

[25] Needless to say, this adjective, which is here synonymous with "mortal", has only
a provisional and indicative function when occurring within the very framework of
contingency.

call an act "sin" which is opposed, first of all, to the divine Nature in one or another of its forms or modes—we have in mind here the divine Qualities and the intrinsic virtues that reflect them—and which, second, in principle engenders posthumous suffering; we say "in principle", for in fact repentance and positive acts on the one hand and divine Mercy on the other efface sins, or can efface them. By a "code of morality" we mean a sacred Legislation insofar as it ordains certain actions and prohibits others, whatever the depth or subtlety with which a particular doctrine may otherwise define its laws; this reservation is necessary because India and the Far East have conceptions of "transgression" and "Law" more finely shaded than those of the Semitic and European West in the sense that, broadly speaking, the compensatory virtue of knowledge is taken into account in the East—"the lustral water without equal", as Hindus say—and because intention plays a much more important part than most Westerners imagine, so that it can even happen, for example, that a guru may prescribe—provisionally and with a view to some particular operation of spiritual alchemy[26]—actions which, while harmful to no one, are contrary to the Law;[27] nonetheless a Legislation does include a moral code, and man as such is so made that he distinguishes, rightly or wrongly, between a "good" and an "evil", which means that his perspective is necessarily fragmentary and analytical. Moreover, when we say that certain acts are opposed to the "divine Nature", we do so with the reservation that metaphysically nothing can be opposed to this Nature; Islam expresses this in affirming that nothing can be separated from the divine Will, not even sin;[28] such ideas are in agreement with non-Semitic perspectives, which always insist strongly on the relativity of phenomena and the variability of definitions according to perspectives.

It is this essential and as it were non-formal conception of sin that explains the absence of an elaborated doctrine of sin in a tra-

[26] Islam is not ignorant of this viewpoint; witness the Koranic story of the mysterious sage who scandalizes his disciple by actions having a secret intention while being outwardly illegal.

[27] Or more precisely to "prescriptions", such as exist in Hinduism and in the West, especially in Judaism; there can be no question of infringements seriously harmful to the collectivity.

[28] Christianity also admits this idea by force of circumstance, but puts less emphasis on it.

dition, such as Shinto, which remains "archaic" and therefore to a large extent "unarticulated"; the rules of purity are the supports of a primordial synthetic virtue, superior to actions and considered as conferring on them a spiritual quality; whereas Semitic morals start from action—outside esoterism at any rate—and seem to confine virtue to the realm of action and even to define it in terms of action, Shinto morality and analogous codes[29] take inward and comprehensive virtue as their starting point and do not see acts as independent and self-contained crystallizations; it is only *a posteriori* and as a consequence of the "externalizing" influence of time that the need for a more analytical code of morality could make itself felt.

Sin, as we have said, retraces the fall. But sin is not the only thing that retraces it within the realm of human attitudes and activities; there are also much subtler, and at the same time less serious, factors which intervene in a well-regulated life and which are connected with what the Arabs call *barakah*; these factors become increasingly important perhaps as the spiritual aim becomes higher. They are connected on the most diverse levels with a choice of things or situations, with the intuition of the spiritual quality of forms, gestures, morally neutral actions; their domain is connected with symbolism, aesthetics, with the significance of materials, proportions, movements—in short with everything that has meaning and importance in a sacred art, a liturgy, a protocol. From a certain point of view all this might seem negligible, but it is no longer at all so when one reflects on the "handling of spiritual influences"—if this expression is permissible—and when one takes account of the fact that there are forms which attract angelic presences whereas there are others which repel them; in the same line of thought, we would say that beside obligations there is also a kind of courtesy toward Heaven. Things have their cosmic relationships and their perfumes, and all things ought to retain something of a recollection of Paradise; life must be lived according to the forms and rhythms of primordial innocence and not according to those of the fall. To act in a way that accords with *barakah* is to act in conformity with a kind of "divine aesthetic": it is an outward application of the "discerning of spirits" or the "science of humors" (*'ilm al-khawâtir* in Arabic),

[29] One might ask whether it is really a question of "morality" in the proper sense, but this is a matter of terminology, which is of little importance to us since we have specified the modes.

as well as of a geometry and a music at once sacred and universal. Everything has a meaning, and everything signifies something; to feel this and to conform to it is to avoid many errors that reason by itself could not prevent. Without this science of *barakah*—this science of "benedictions"—sacred art, which enfolds and penetrates the whole of human existence in traditional civilizations and which even constitutes all that is understood in our day by "culture", at least insofar as these civilizations are concerned, would remain unintelligible, as would all forms of civility, and would have neither meaning nor value.

What matters to the man who is virtually liberated from the fall is to remain in holy infancy. In a certain sense, Adam and Eve were "children" before the fall and became "adult" only through it and after it; the adult age in fact reflects the reign of the fall; old age, in which the passions are silenced, once again brings one near to infancy and Paradise, at least in normal spiritual conditions. The innocence and trust of the very young must be combined with the detachment and resignation of the old; the two ages rejoin one another in contemplativity and then in nearness to God: infancy is "still" close to Him, and old age is so "already". The child can find his happiness in a flower, and so can the old man; extremes meet, and the spiraling circle is closed in Mercy.

The Dialogue between Hellenists and Christians

Like most inter-traditional polemics, the dialogue which opposed Hellenism to Christianity was to a great extent unreal. The fact that each was right on a certain plane—or in a particular "spiritual dimension"—resulted in each emerging as victor in its own way: Christianity by imposing itself on the whole Western world, and Hellenism by surviving in the very heart of Christianity and conferring on Christian intellectuality an indelible imprint.

The misunderstandings were nonetheless profound, and it is not difficult to see why this was so if divergences of perspective are taken into account. From the point of view of the Hellenists, the divine Principle is at the same time one and multiple; the gods personify the divine qualities and functions and, at the same time, the angelic prolongations of these qualities and functions; the idea of immanence prevails over that of transcendence, at least in exoterism. The universe is an order that is so to speak architectural, deployed from the Supreme Principle by way of intermediaries, or of hierarchies of intermediaries, down to earthly creatures; all the cosmic principles and their rays are divine, or semi-divine, which amounts to saying that they are envisaged in relation to their essential and functional divinity. If God gives us life, warmth, and light, He does so by way of Helios or inasmuch as He is Helios; the sun is like the hand of God, and is thus divine; and since it is so in principle, why should it not be so in its sensible manifestation? This way of looking at things is based on the essential continuity between the Cause and the effect, and not on an existential discontinuity or accidentality; the world being the necessary and strictly ordered manifestation of Divinity, it is, like Divinity, eternal; it is, for God, a way of deploying Himself "outside Himself". This eternity does not imply that the world cannot undergo eclipses, but if it inevitably does so, as all mythologies teach, it is so that it may rise again in accordance with an eternal rhythm; it therefore cannot not be. The very absoluteness of the Absolute necessitates relativity; *Mâyâ* is "without origin", say the Vedantists. There is no "gratuitous creation" nor any creation *ex nihilo*; there is a necessary manifestation *ex divino*, and this manifestation is free within the framework of its necessity, and necessary within the framework of its liberty. The world is divine through its character as a divine manifestation, or by way of the metaphysical marvel of its existence.

There is no need to describe here, on account of a concern for symmetry, the Christian outlook, which is that of Semitic monotheism and is for that reason familiar to everyone. On the other hand, it seems indispensable before proceeding further to clarify the fact that the Hellenistic conception of the "divinity of the world" has nothing to do with the error of pantheism, for the cosmic manifestation of God in no way detracts from the absolute transcendence appertaining to the Principle in itself, and in no way contradicts what is metaphysically acceptable in the Semitic and Christian conception of a *creatio ex nihilo*. To believe that the world is a "part" of God and that God, by His Selfhood or by His very essence, spreads Himself into the forms of the world, would be a truly "pagan" conception—such as has no doubt existed here and there, even among the men of old—and in order to keep clear of it, one must possess a knowledge that is intrinsically what would be represented on the plane of ideas by a combination between the Hellenistic "cosmosophy" and the Judeo-Christian theology, the reciprocal relationship of these two outlooks playing the part of a touchstone with respect to total truth. Metaphysically speaking, the Semitic and monotheistic "creationism", as soon as it presents itself as an absolute and exclusive truth, is nearly as false as pantheism; it is so "metaphysically", because total knowledge is in question and not the opportuneness of salvation alone, and "nearly" because a half-truth which tends to safeguard the transcendence of God at the expense of the metaphysical intelligibility of the world is less erroneous than a half-truth which tends to safeguard the divine nature of the world at the expense of the intelligibility of God.

If the Christian polemicists did not understand that the outlook of the Greek sages was no more than the esoteric complement of the Biblical notion of creation, the Greek polemicists did not understand the compatibility between the two outlooks any better. It is true that one incomprehension sometimes begets another, for it is difficult to penetrate the profound intention of a strange concept when that intention remains implicit, and when in addition it is presented as destined to replace truths which are perhaps partial, but which are in any case evident to those who accept them traditionally. A partial truth may be insufficient from one point of view or another; it is nonetheless a truth.

*　　*　　*

In order properly to understand the significance of this dialogue, which in some respects was but a confrontation between two monologues, one must take account of the following: as far as the Christians were concerned there was no knowledge possible without love; that is to say that in their eyes *gnosis* was valid only on condition that it was included within a unifying experience; by itself, and apart from the living experience of spiritual reality, an intellectual knowledge of the Universe had no meaning to them; but eventually the Christians had to recognize the rights of a knowledge that was theoretical, and thus conceptual and proleptic, which they did by borrowing from the Greeks certain elements of their science, not without sometimes heaping abuse on Hellenism as such, with as much ingratitude as inconsistency. If a simple and rather summary formulation be permissible, one could say that for the Greeks truth is that which is in conformity with the nature of things; for the Christians truth is that which leads to God. This Christian attitude, to the extent that it tended to be exclusive, was bound to appear to the Greeks as "foolishness"; in the eyes of the Christians the attitude of the Greeks consisted in taking thought for an end in itself, outside of any personal relation to God; consequently it was a "wisdom according to the flesh", since it cannot by itself regenerate the fallen and impotent will, but on the contrary by its self-sufficiency draws men away from the thirst for God and for salvation. From the Greek point of view, things are what they are whatever we may make of them; from the Christian—to speak schematically and *a priori*—only our relationship to God makes sense. The Christians could be reproached for an outlook that was too much concerned with the will and too self-interested, and the Greeks on the one hand for too much liveliness of thought and on the other for too rational and too human a perfectionism; it was in some respects a dispute between a love-song and a mathematical theorem. It could also be said that the Hellenists were predominantly right in principle and the Christians in fact, at least in a particular sense that can be discerned without difficulty.

As for the Christian gnostics, they necessarily admitted the doctrinal anticipations of the divine mysteries, but on condition—it cannot be too strongly emphasized—that they remained in a quasi-organic connection with the spiritual experience of *gnosis*-love; to know God is to love Him, or rather, since the Scriptural point of departure is love: to love God perfectly is to know Him. To know was indeed *a priori* to conceive of supernatural truths, but to do so while making our whole being participate in this understanding; it was thus to love the divine quintessence of all *gnosis*, that quintessence which is "love" because it is at once union and beatitude. The school of Alexandria was as fully Christian as that of Antioch, in the sense that it saw in the acceptance of Christ the *sine qua non* of salvation; its foundations were perfectly Pauline. In Saint Paul's view a conceptual and expressible *gnosis* is a knowing "in part" (*ex parte*), and it shall be "done away" when "that which is perfect is come",[1] namely, the totality of *gnosis*, which, through the very fact of its totality, is "love" (*caritas*, ἀγάπη[*]), the divine prototype of human *gnosis*. In the case of man there is a distinction—or a complementarism—between love and knowledge, but in God their polarity is surpassed and unified. In the Christian perspective this supreme degree is called "love", but in another perspective—notably in the Vedantic—one can equally well call it "knowledge", while maintaining, not that knowledge finds its totalization or its exaltation in love, but on the contrary that love (*bhakti*), being individual, finds its sublimation in pure knowledge (*jnâna*), which is universal; this second mode of expression is directly in conformity with the sapiential perspective.

*   *   *

The Christian protest is unquestionably justified insofar as it is directed to the "humanist" side of "classical" Hellenism and to the mystical ineffectuality of philosophy as such. On the other hand, it is in no way logical to reproach the Greeks with a divinization of the cosmos on the pretext that there can be no "entry" of God into the world, while admitting that Christ, and he alone, brings about just such an entry; indeed, if Christ can bring it about, it is precisely because it is possible and because it is realized *a priori* by the cosmos itself; the "avataric" marvel of Christ retraces, or humanizes, the cosmic marvel of creation or of "emanation".

---

[1] 1 Corinthians 13:10.
[*] Translator's note: *agapê* in English transliteration.

From the point of view of the Platonists—in the widest sense—
the return to God is inherent in the fact of existence: our being
itself offers the way of return, for that being is divine in its nature,
otherwise it would be nothing; that is why we must return, passing
through the strata of our ontological reality, all the way to pure Substance, which is one; it is thus that we become perfectly "ourselves".
Man realizes what he knows: a full comprehension—in the light of
the Absolute—of relativity dissolves it and leads back to the Absolute.
Here again there is no irreducible antagonism between Greeks and
Christians: if the intervention of Christ can become necessary, it is
not because deliverance is something other than a return, through
the strata of our own being, to our true Self, but because the function of Christ is to render such a return possible. It is made possible
on two planes, the one existential and exoteric and the other intellectual and esoteric; the second plane is hidden in the first, which
alone appears in the full light of day, and that is the reason why for
the common run of mortals the Christian perspective is only existential and separative, not intellectual and unitive. This gives rise to
another misunderstanding between Christians and Platonists: while
the Platonists propound liberation by Knowledge because man is
an intelligence,[2] the Christians envisage in their general doctrine a
salvation by Grace because man is an existence—as such separated
from God—and a fallen and impotent will. Once again, the Greeks
can be reproached for having at their disposal but a single way, inaccessible in fact to the majority, and for giving the impression that
it is philosophy that saves, just as one can reproach the Christians
for ignoring liberation by Knowledge and for assigning an absolute
character to our existential and volitive reality alone and to the
means appropriate to that aspect of our being, or for taking into
consideration our existential relativity alone and not our "intellectual absoluteness"; nevertheless the reproach to the Greeks cannot
concern their sages, any more than the reproach to the Christians
can impugn their *gnosis*, nor in a general way their sanctity.

[2] Islam, in conformity with its "paracletic" character, reflects this point of view—
which is also that of the *Vedânta* and of all other forms of *gnosis*—in a Semitic and
religious mode, and realizes it all the more readily in its esoterism; like the Hel-
lenist, the Muslim asks first of all: "What must I know or admit, seeing that I have
an intelligence capable of objectivity and of totality?" and not *a priori*: "What must
I want, since I have a will that is free, but fallen?"

The possibility of our return to God—wherein are different degrees—is universal and timeless: it is inscribed in the very nature of our existence and of our intelligence; our powerlessness can only be accidental, not essential. That which is principially indispensable is an intervention of the *Logos*, but not in every case the intervention of a particular manifestation of the *Logos*, unless we belong to it by reason of our situation and, by virtue of that fact, it chooses us; as soon as it chooses us, it holds the place of the Absolute as far as we are concerned, and then it "is" the Absolute. It could even be said that the imperative character that Christ assumes for Christians—or for men providentially destined for Christianity—retraces the imperative character inherent in the *Logos* in every spiritual way, whether of the West or of the East.

*   *   *

One must react against the evolutionist prejudice which would have it that the thought of the Greeks "attained" to a certain level or a certain result, that is to say, that the triad Socrates-Plato-Aristotle represents the summit of an entirely "natural" thought, a summit reached after long periods of effort and groping. The reverse is the truth, in the sense that all the said triad did was to crystallize rather imperfectly a primordial and intrinsically timeless wisdom, actually of Aryan origin and typologically close to the Celtic, Germanic, Mazdean, and Brahmanic esoterisms. There is in Aristotelian rationality and even in the Socratic dialectic a sort of "humanism" more or less connected with artistic naturalism and scientific curiosity, and thus with empiricism. But this already too contingent dialectic—though we must bear in mind that the Socratic dialogues belong to spiritual "pedagogy" and have something of the provisional in them—must not lead us into attributing a "natural" character to intellections that are "supernatural" by definition, or "naturally supernatural". On the whole, Plato expressed sacred truths in a language that had already become profane—profane because more rational and discursive than intuitive and symbolist, or because it followed too closely the contingencies and humors of the mirror that is the mind—whereas Aristotle placed truth itself, and not merely its expression, on a profane and "humanistic" plane. The originality of Aristotle and his school resides no doubt in giving to truth a maximum of rational bases, but this cannot be done without diminishing that truth, and it has no purpose save where there is a regression of intellectual intuition; it is a "two-edged sword" precisely because truth seems henceforth to be at the mercy of syllogisms. The question of knowing whether this constitutes a betrayal or a providential readaptation is of small importance here, and could no doubt be answered in either sense.[3] What is certain is that Aristotle's teaching, so far as its essential content is concerned, is still much too true to be understood and appreciated by the protagonists of the "dynamic" and relativist or "existentialist" thought of our epoch. This last half-plebeian, half-demonic kind of thought is in contradiction with itself from its very point of departure, since to say that everything is relative or "dynamic", and therefore "in motion", is to say that there exists no point of view from which that fact can be established; Aristotle had in any case fully foreseen this absurdity.

The moderns have reproached the pre-Socratic philosophers—and all the sages of the East as well—with trying to construct a picture of the universe without asking themselves whether our faculties of knowledge are equal to such an enterprise; the reproach is perfectly vain, for the very fact that we can put such a question proves that our intelligence is in principle adequate to the needs of the case. It is not the "dogmatists" who are naive, but the skeptics, who have not the least idea in the world of what is implicit in the "dogmatism" they oppose. In our day some people go so far as to claim that the goal of philosophy can only be the search for a "type of rationality"

---

[3] With Pythagoras one is still in the Aryan East; with Socrates-Plato one is no longer wholly in that East—which in reality is neither "Eastern" nor "Western", that distinction having no meaning for an archaic Europe—but neither is one wholly in the West; whereas with Aristotle Europe begins to become specifically "Western" in the current and cultural sense of the word. The East—or a particular East—forced an entry with Christianity, but the Aristotelian and Caesarean West finally prevailed, only to escape in the end from both Aristotle and Caesar, but by the downward path. It is opportune to observe here that all modern theological attempts to "surpass" the teaching of Aristotle can follow only the same downward path, in view of the falsity of their motives, whether implicit or explicit. What is really being sought is a graceful capitulation before evolutionist scientism, before the machine, before an activist and demagogic socialism, a destructive psychologism, abstract art and surrealism, in short before modernism in all its forms—that modernism which is less and less a "humanism" since it de-humanizes, or that individualism which is ever more infra-individual. The moderns, who are neither Pythagoreans nor Vedantists, are surely the last to have any right to complain of Aristotle.

adapted to the comprehension of "human reality"; the error is the same, but a coarser and meaner version of it, and more insolent as well. How is it that they cannot see that the very idea of inventing an intelligence capable of resolving such problems proves, in the first place, that this intelligence exists already—for it alone could conceive of any such idea—and shows in the second place that the goal aimed at is of an unfathomable absurdity? But our present purpose is not to prolong this subject; it is simply to call attention to the parallelism between the pre-Socratic—or more precisely the Ionian—wisdom and Oriental doctrines such as the *Vaisheshika* and the *Sânkhya*, and to underline, on the one hand, that in all these ancient visions of the Universe the implicit postulate is the innateness of the nature of things in the Intellect[4] and not a supposition or other logical operation, and on the other hand, that this notion of innateness furnishes the very definition of that which the skeptics and empiricists think they must disdainfully characterize as "dogmatism"; in this way they demonstrate that they are ignorant, not only of the nature of intellection, but also of the nature of dogmas in the proper sense of the word. The admirable thing about the Platonists is not, to be sure, their "thought"; it is the content of their thought, whether called "dogmatic" or otherwise.

The Sophists inaugurate the era of individualistic rationalism and unlimited pretensions; thus they open the door to all arbitrary totalitarianisms. It is true that profane philosophy also begins with Aristotle, but in a rather different sense, since the rationality of the Stagirite tends upwards and not downwards, as does that of Protagoras and his like; in other words, if a dissipating individualism originates with the Sophists—not forgetting allied spirits such as Democritus and Epicurus—Aristotle on the other hand opens the era of a rationalism still anchored in metaphysical certitude, but nonetheless fragile and ambiguous in its very principle, as there has more than once been occasion to point out.

However that may be, if one wants to understand the Christian reaction, one must take account of all these aspects of the spirit of Greece, and at the same time of the Biblical, mystical, and "real-

---

[4] In the terminology of the ancient cosmologists one must allow for symbolism: when Thales saw in "water" the origin of all things, we have every reason to believe that it is the Universal Substance—the *Prakriti* of the Hindus—that is in question and not the sensible element. It is the same with the "air" of Anaximenes of Miletus or of Diogenes of Apollonia, or with the "fire" of Heraclitus.

izational" character of Christianity. Greek thought appeared in the main as a Promethean attempt to appropriate to itself the light of Heaven, rashly breaking through the stages on the way to Truth; but at the same time it was largely irresistible because of the self-evidence of its content: that being so, one must not lose sight of the fact that in the East sapiential doctrines were never presented in the form of a "literature" open to all, but that on the contrary their assimilation required a corresponding spiritual method, and this is the very thing that had disappeared and could no longer be found among the Greeks of the classical epoch.

*   *   *

It has been said and said again that the Hellenists and the Orientals—"Platonic" spirits in the widest sense—have been blameworthy in "arrogantly" rejecting Christ, or that they are trying to escape from their "responsibilities"—once again and always!—as creatures toward the Creator in withdrawing into their own center where they claim to find, in their own pure being, the essence of things and the divine Reality; they thus dilute, it is alleged, the quality of creature and at the same time that of Creator with a sort of pantheistic impersonalism, which amounts to saying that they destroy the relationship of "obligation" between the Creator and the creature. In reality "responsibilities" are relative as we ourselves are relative in our existential particularity; they cannot be less relative—or "more absolute"—than the subject to which they are related. One who, by the grace of Heaven, succeeds in escaping from the tyranny of the ego is by that very circumstance discharged from the responsibilities that the ego entails. God shows Himself as creative Person insofar as—or in relation to the fact that—we are "creature" and individual, but that particular reciprocal relationship is far from exhausting all our ontological and intellectual nature; that is to say, our nature cannot be exhaustively defined by notions of "duty", of "rights", nor by other fixations of the kind. It has been said that the "rejection" of the Christic gift on the part of the "Platonic" spirit constitutes the subtlest and most luciferian perversity of the intelligence; this argument, born of a misguided instinct of self-preservation, though understandable on its own plane, can easily and far more pertinently be turned against those who make use of it: for if we are obliged at all costs to find some mental perversion somewhere, we shall find it with those who want to substitute for the Absolute a personal and therefore relative God, and temporal phenomena for metaphysical principles, not in connection with a childlike faith making no demands of anyone, but within the framework of the most exacting erudition and the most totalitarian intellectual pretension. If there is such a thing as abuse of the intelligence, it is to be found in the substitution of the relative for the Absolute, or the accident for the Substance, on the pretext of putting the "concrete" above the "abstract";[5] it is not to be found in the rejection—in the name of transcendent and immutable principles—of a relativity presented as absoluteness.

The misunderstanding between Christians and Hellenists can in large part be condensed to a false alternative: in effect, the fact that God resides in our deepest "being"—or in the transpersonal depth of our consciousness—and that we can in principle realize Him with the help of the pure and theomorphic Intellect, in no way excludes the equal and simultaneous affirmation of this immanent and impersonal Divinity as objective and personal, nor the fact that we can do nothing without His grace, despite the essentially "divine" character of the Intellect in which we participate naturally and supernaturally.

It is perfectly true that the human individual is a concrete and definite person, and responsible before a Creator, a personal and omniscient Legislator; but it is quite as true—to say the least of it— that man is but a modality, so to speak external and coagulated, of a Divinity at once impersonal and personal, and that human intelligence is such that it can in principle be conscious of this fact and thus realize its true identity. In one sense it is evidently the fallen and sinful individuality that is "ourselves"; in another sense it is the transcendent and unalterable Self: the planes are different; there is no common measure between them.

When the religious dogmatist claims for some terrestrial fact an absolute import—and the "relatively absolute" character of the same fact is not here in question—the Platonist or the Oriental appeals to principial and timeless certitudes; in other words, when the dogmatist asserts that "this is", the gnostic immediately asks: "By

---

[5] It is really an abuse of language to qualify as "abstract" everything that is above the phenomenal order.

virtue of what possibility?" According to the gnostic, "everything has already been"; he admits the "new" only insofar as it retraces or manifests the "ancient", or rather the timeless, uncreated "idea". The function of celestial messages is in practice and humanly absolute, but they are not for that reason the Absolute, and as far as their form is concerned they do not pass beyond relativity. It is the same with the intellect at once "created" and "uncreated": the "uncreated" element penetrates it as light penetrates air or ether; this element is not the light, but is its vehicle, and in practice one cannot dissociate them.

There are two sources of certitude: on the one hand the innateness of the Absolute in pure intelligence, and on the other the supernatural phenomenon of grace. It is amply evident—and cannot be too often repeated—that these two sources can be, and consequently must be, combined to a certain extent, but in fact the exoterists have an interest in setting them against each other, and they do so by denying to intelligence its supernatural essence and by denying the innateness of the Absolute, as well as by denying grace to those who think differently from themselves. An irreducible opposition between intellection and grace is as artificial as it could be, for intellection is also a grace, but it is a static and innate grace; there can be absolutely no reason why this kind of grace should not be a possibility and should never be manifested, seeing that by its very nature it cannot not be. If anyone objects that in such matters it is not a matter of "grace" but something else, the answer must be that in that case grace is not necessary, since there are only two alternatives: either grace is indispensable, and if so intellection is a grace, or intellection is not a grace, and if so grace is not indispensable.

If theologians admit, with the Scriptures, that one cannot enunciate an essential truth about Christ "but by the Holy Spirit", they must also admit that one cannot enunciate an essential truth about God without the intervention of that same Spirit; the truths of the wisdom of Greece, like the metaphysical truths of all peoples, are therefore not to be robbed of their "supernatural" and in principle salvific character.

From a certain point of view, the Christian argument is the historicity of the Christ-Savior, whereas the Platonic or "Aryan" argument is the nature of things or the Immutable. If, to speak symbolically, all men are in danger of drowning as a consequence of the fall of Adam, the Christian saves himself by grasping the pole held out to him by Christ, which no one else can hold out, whereas the Platonist saves himself by swimming; but neither course weakens or neutralizes the effectiveness of the other. On the one hand there are certainly men who do not know how to swim or who are prevented from doing so, but on the other hand swimming is undeniably among the possibilities open to man; the whole thing is to know what counts most in a situation whether individual or collective.[6] We have seen that Hellenism, like all directly or indirectly sapiential doctrines, is founded on the axiom man-intelligence rather than man-will, and that is one of the reasons why it had to appear as inoperative in the eyes of a majority of Christians; but only "of a majority" because the Christian gnostics could not apply such a reproach to the Pythagoreans and Platonists; the gnostics could not do otherwise than admit the primacy of the Intellect, and for that reason the idea of divine redemption meant to them something very different from and more far-reaching than a mysticism derived from history and a sacramental dogmatism. It is necessary to repeat once more—as others have said before and better—that sacred facts are true because they retrace on their own plane the nature of things, and not the other way round: the nature of things is not real or normative because it evokes certain sacred facts. The principles, essentially accessible to pure intelligence—if they were not so man would not be man, and it is almost blasphemy to deny that human intelligence considered in relation to animal intelligence has a supernatural side—the universal principles confirm the sacred facts, which in their turn reflect those principles and derive their efficacy from them; it is not history, whatever it may contain, that confirms the principles. This relationship is expressed by the Buddhists when they say that spiritual truth is situated beyond the distinction between objectivity and subjectivity, and that it derives its evidence from the depths of Being itself, or from the innateness of Truth in all that is.

In the sapiential perspective divine redemption is always present; it pre-exists all terrestrial alchemy and is its celestial model, so that it is always thanks to this eternal redemption—whatever may be its

---

[6] In other words: if one party cannot logically deny that there are men who save themselves by swimming, no more can the other party deny that there are men who are saved only because a pole is held out to them.

vehicle on earth—that man is freed from the weight of his vagaries and even, *Deo volente,* from that of his separative existence; if "my words shall not pass away" it is because they have always been. The Christ of the gnostics is he who is "before Abraham was" and from whom arise all the ancient wisdoms; a consciousness of this, far from diminishing a participation in the treasures of the historical Redemption, confers on them a scope that touches the very roots of Existence.

American Indian Shamanism

By "Shamanism" we mean traditions of "prehistoric" origin that are characteristic of Mongoloid peoples, including the American Indians;[1] in Asia we encounter this Shamanism properly so called not only in Siberia, but also in Tibet—in the form of *Bön*—and in Mongolia, Manchuria, and Korea; pre-Buddhist Chinese tradition, with its Confucian and Taoist branches, is also connected to this traditional family, and the same applies to Japan, where Shamanism has given rise to the particular tradition of Shinto. All these doctrines are characterized by a complementary opposition between Earth and Heaven as well as by a worship of Nature, which is envisaged in relation to its essential causality and not its existential accidentality; they are also distinguished by a certain parsimony in their eschatology—quite apparent even in Confucianism—and above all by the central function of the shaman, assumed in China by the *Tao-tse*[2] and in Tibet by the lamas concerned with divination and exorcism.[3] If we mention China and Japan here, it is not to incorporate their indigenous traditions summarily into Siberian Shamanism, but to indicate the place they occupy in relation to the primitive tradition of the yellow race, a tradition of which Shamanism is the most direct—though also, it must be admitted, the most uneven and ambiguous—continuation.

This last remark raises the question of knowing the spiritual value of the Siberian and American forms of Shamanism; the general impression is that one finds the very widest differences of level, but what is certain is that among the American Indians—for it is of them that we shall be speaking here—something primordial and pure has been preserved despite all the obscurations that may have been superimposed in certain tribes, perhaps mostly in relatively recent times.

---

[1] But not the Mexicans and Peruvians, who represent later traditional filiations— "Atlanteans", according to a certain terminology—and who therefore no longer spring from the aerie of the "Thunderbird".

[2] Not to be confused with the *Tao-shi*, who are contemplative monks.

[3] The demarcation between *Bön* and Lamaism is not always clear, each tradition having influenced the other.

Documents bearing testimony to the spiritual quality of the American Indians are numerous. A white man who was captured by them in his early infancy—at the beginning of the nineteenth century—and who lived until his twentieth year among tribes (Kickapoo, Kansas, Omaha, Osage) that had never had the slightest contact with a missionary, says: "It is certain that they acknowledge—at least as far as my acquaintance extends—one supreme, all powerful, and intelligent Being, or Giver of Life, who created and governs all things. They believe in general that, after the hunting grounds had been formed and supplied with game, He created the first red man and woman, who were very large in their stature and lived to an exceeding old age; that He often held councils and smoked with them, gave them laws to be obeyed, and taught them how to take game and cultivate corn: but that in consequence of their disobedience, He withdrew from and abandoned them to the vexations of the Evil Spirit, who has since been the cause of all their degeneracy and sufferings. They believe the Great Spirit of too exalted a character to be directly the author of evil, and that He continues to shower down on His red children—despite their offences—all the blessings they enjoy; in response to this parental solicitude, they are truly filial and sincere in their devotions, praying to Him for such things as they need and returning thanks for what they have received. In all the tribes I have visited, I have found a belief in a future life with rewards and punishments. . . . This conviction concerning their accountability to the Great Spirit makes the Indians generally scrupulous and fervent in their traditional beliefs and observances, and it is a fact worthy of remark that one finds among them neither frigidity, indifference, nor hypocrisy in regard to sacred things."[4]

Another testimony, coming this time from a Christian source, is as follows: "Belief in a supreme Being is firmly rooted in the culture of the Chippewas. This Being, called *Kîchê Manitô*, or Great Spirit, was far removed from them. Prayers were rarely addressed directly to Him alone and sacrifices were only offered to Him at the feast of the Midewiwin initiates. My informants spoke of Him in a tone of submission and extreme reverence. 'He has placed all things on earth and takes care of everything,' added an old man, the most powerful medicine-man of the Short Ear Lake Reservation. One

[4] John D. Hunter, *Manners and Customs of Indian Tribes* (Minneapolis, 1957).

elderly woman of the same reservation stated that when praying the Indians of old first of all addressed *Kîchê Manitô* and afterwards 'the other great spirits, the *kitchî manitô*, who live in the winds, the snow, the thunder, the tempest, the trees, and in all things'. One aged shaman called Vermilion was convinced that 'all the Indians in this country knew God long before the arrival of the Whites; but they did not ask Him for particular things as they do now that they have become Christians. They expected favors from their own special protectors'. Less powerful than *Kîchê Manitô* were the divinities inhabiting Nature and also the guardian spirits. . . . The belief of the Chippewas in a life after death is made plain by their burial and mourning customs, but they have a tradition that souls after death go toward the West, 'toward the place the sun sets' or 'toward the prairies which contain the camping-grounds of blessing and eternal happiness'".[5]

Since our point of view is not that of evolutionism, to say the least, we cannot believe in a crude and pluralistic origin of religions, and we have no reason to cast doubt on the "monotheistic" aspect

---

[5] Sister M. Inez Hilger, *Chippewa Child Life and Its Cultural Background* (Washington, 1951). "Religion was the veritable life of the tribes, penetrating all their activities and all their institutions. . . . Concerning the Indians of North America the most surprising fact, which has been taken into account too late, is that they lived customarily in and by religion, to a degree comparable to the piety of the ancient Israelites under their theocracy" (Garrick Mallery, *Picture Writing of the American Indians, 10: Annual Report of the Bureau of Ethnography* [1893]). An author who lived for 60 years among the Choctaw wrote: "I claim for the Indian of North America the purest religion and the loftiest conceptions of the Great Creator" (John James, *My Experience with the Indians* [1925]). "To call all these people simply religious gives but a faint idea of the profound attitude of piety and devotion that penetrates all their conduct. Their honesty is immaculate, and their purity of intention such that their observances of the rites of their religion suffer no exception and are extremely remarkable. They are certainly closer to a nation of saints than a horde of savages" (Washington Irving, *The Adventures of Captain Bonneville* [1837]). "*Tirawa* is an intangible, all-powerful, and beneficent Spirit. He penetrates the Universe, and He is the supreme sovereign. Upon His will depends everything that happens. He may lead to good or evil; He may give success or failure. Everything is done with Him. . . . Nothing is undertaken without a prayer to the Father for help" (George Bird Grinnel, "Pawnee Mythology", *Journal of American Folklore*, Vol. VI). "The Blackfeet believe firmly in the Supernatural and in the control of human affairs by the good or evil Powers of the invisible world. The Great Spirit, or Great Mystery, or Good Power, is everywhere and in all things" (Walter McClintock, *The Old North Trail*, [London, 1910]).

of the tradition of the Indians,[6] especially since "polytheism" pure and simple is never anything but a degeneration, hence a relatively late phenomenon, and in any case much less widespread than is ordinarily supposed. Primordial monotheism, which has nothing specifically Semitic about it and is best described as a "pan-mono-theism"—otherwise polytheism could not have been derived from it—subsists or has left its trace among peoples of the most diverse kind, including the Pygmies of Africa; theologians call this "primi-tive religion". In the Americas, the Fuegians for instance know only a single God dwelling beyond the stars, who has no body and does not sleep and for whom the stars serve as eyes; He has always been and will never die; He created the world and gave rules of action to men. Among the Indians of North America—those of the Plains and of the Forests—the divine Unity is no doubt less exclusively affirmed and in some cases even seems to be veiled, and yet among these peoples nothing is to be found strictly comparable to the anthropomorphic polytheism of the ancient Europeans; it is true that there are several "Great Powers",[7] but these Powers are either subordinated to a supreme Power resembling *Brahma* much more than Jupiter, or they are regarded as a totality or as a supernatural Substance of which we ourselves are parts, as was explained to us by a Sioux. In order to understand this last point, which would represent pantheism if the entire concept were reduced to this formulation, one must know that ideas concerning the Great Spirit are connected either to the "discontinuous" reality of the Essence, which implies a transcendentalism,[8] or to the "continuous" reality

---

[6] In 1770 a woman visionary announced to the Oglala Sioux that the Great Spirit was angry with them; in the pictographic narratives ("winter counts") of the Oglala, this year was given the name *Wakan Tanka knashkiyan* ("Great Spirit in anger"); now this happened at a time when the Sioux could not have come under the influence of white monotheism.

[7] The name *Wakan Tanka*—literally "Great Sacred" (*wakan* = sacred) and com-monly translated "Great Spirit" or "Great Mystery"—has also been rendered "Great Powers", the plural being justified in view of the polysynthetic meaning of the concept. In any case it is not without reason that the Sioux have been called "the Unitarians of the American Indians".

[8] It goes without saying that we are using this word in its proper sense and with no thought of the Emersonian philosophy known by this name. One might wonder—it may be said in passing—whether Emerson's works do not reveal, besides his German idealism, a certain influence coming from the Indians.

of the Substance, which implies a panentheism; in the consciousness of the American Indians, however, the relation of Substance has more importance than that of Essence. One sometimes hears of a magical Power animating all things, including men, called *Manito* (Algonquin) or *Orenda* (Iroquois), which is coagulated—or personified, according to the case—in things and beings, including those that belong to the invisible and animistic world, and which also becomes crystallized in connection with some human subject as a totem or "guardian angel" (the *orayon* of the Iroquois);[9] all this is correct, with the reservation however that the qualification "magical" is quite insufficient and even erroneous in the sense that it defines a cause in terms of a partial effect. Be that as it may, the important thing to remember is that Indian theism, while it is not a pluralism of the Mediterranean and "pagan" type, does not coincide exactly either with Abrahamic monotheism, but represents rather a somewhat "fluid" theosophy—in the absence of a sacred Scripture—akin to Vedic and Far-Eastern conceptions; it is also important to note the emphasis in this perspective on the aspects of "life" and "power", which is entirely characteristic of a warlike and more or less nomadic mentality.

Certain tribes—the Algonquins especially and the Iroquois—distinguish between the demiurge and the supreme Spirit; the demiurge often assumes a role that borders on the burlesque, even the luciferian. Such a conception of the creative Power, and of the primordial dispenser of arts, is far from being confined to the American Indians, as is proven by the mythologies of the Ancient World where the misdeeds of the Titans stand side by side with those of the gods; in Biblical terms, we would say that there is no terrestrial Paradise without its serpent and that without the serpent there could be no fall and no human drama, nor any reconciliation with Heaven. Since the creation is in any case something that distances itself from God, a deifugal tendency must necessarily be inherent in it, so much so that it can be considered under two aspects, one divine and the other demiurgic or luciferian; now the Indians mingle these two aspects, and they are not alone in doing so; one need only recall the case of the god Susano-o in Japanese mythology, the turbulent genius of sea and storm. In short, the

---

[9] On the whole this is equivalent to the *kami* of Shintoism.

demiurge—the *Nanabozho, Mishabo,* and *Napi* of the Algonquins, and the *Tharonhiawagon* of the Iroquois—is none other than *Mâyâ*, the protean principle which encompasses at once the creative Power and the world and which is *natura naturans* as well as *natura naturata*; *Mâyâ* is beyond good and evil, expressing both plenitude and privation, the divine and the all too human, even the titanic and the demonic: an ambiguity that sentimental moralism finds it difficult to understand.

As far as cosmogony is concerned, there is hardly anything of a *creatio ex nihilo* for the Indian; there is instead a sort of transformation. In a celestial world situated above the visible sky, there lived in the beginning semi-divine beings, the prototypical and normative personages whom earthly man must imitate in all things; and there was only peace in this celestial world. But a time came when some of these beings sowed the seeds of discord, and then occurred the great change; they were exiled upon the earth and became the ancestors of all earthly creatures; some were able to remain in Heaven, however, and these are the geniuses of every essential activity, such as hunting, war, love, cultivation. According to the Indian, what we call "creation" is above all a change of state or a descent; this implies an "emanationist" perspective—in the positive and legitimate sense of the word—which is here explained by the predominance among the Indians of the idea of Substance, hence a "non-discontinuous" Reality. This is the perspective of the spiral or star, not that of concentric circles, although this latter perspective of discontinuity must never be lost from view; the two perspectives are complementary, but the accent is sometimes on one and sometimes on the other.

What is the correct and concrete meaning of the Indian idea that everything is "animated"? In principle and metaphysically it means that there springs forth from each thing—from its existential center—an ontological ray that is made of "being", "consciousness", "life", a ray which connects the object through its subtle or animistic root to its luminous and celestial prototype; from this it follows that it is possible for us to attain to the heavenly Essences by taking anything whatever as starting point. Things are coagulations of the divine Substance; the Substance is not things, but things are it, and they are so by virtue of their existence and their qualities; this is the profound meaning of the polysynthetic animism of the Indians, and it is this acute consciousness of the homogeneity of the phenomenal world that explains their spiritual naturalism and also their refusal to detach themselves from nature and to become involved in a civilization made up of artifices and servitudes and carrying within itself the seeds of petrifaction as well as corruption; for the Indian as for the Far-Easterner, the human is within nature and not outside it.

*   *   *

The most eminent manifestations of the Great Spirit are the cardinal points together with the Zenith and Nadir, or Heaven and Earth, and then such forms as the Sun, the Morning Star, the Rock, the Eagle, the Bison; all these manifestations are within ourselves while their roots subsist in Divinity: although the Great Spirit is One, It comprises within Itself all those qualities whose traces we see—and whose effects we experience—in the world of appearances.[10]

The East is Light and Knowledge as well as Peace; the South is Warmth and Life, hence Growth and Happiness; the West is fertilizing Water as well as Revelation speaking in lightning and thunder; the North is Cold and Purity, or Strength. Thus it is that the Universe, at whatever level considered—Earth, Man, or Heaven—depends on four primordial determinations: Light, Heat, Water, and Cold. What is remarkable about this way of describing the cardinal points is that they do not expressly symbolize either the four elements—air, fire, water, earth—or their corresponding physical states—dryness, heat, moisture, cold—but rather mix or combine the two quaternaries unequally: North and South are characterized respectively

---

[10] Sages among the Indians are by no means ignorant of the contingent and illusory character of the cosmos: "I saw more than I can tell, and I understood more than I saw; for I was seeing in a sacred manner the shapes of all things in the spirit and the shape of all shapes as they must live together like one being. . . . Crazy Horse dreamed and went into the world where there is nothing but the spirits of all things. That is the real world that is behind this one, and everything we see here is something like a shadow from that world. . . . I knew the real was yonder and the darkened dream of it was here" (Black Elk [Hehaka Sapa], in *Black Elk Speaks* [Lincoln, 1961]). [Translator's note: the most recent edition is *Black Elk Speaks* (Lincoln, Nebraska: University of Nebraska, 2000).] According to Hartley Burr Alexander, "The fundamental idea (of the Mexican myth of Quetzalcoatl) is the same (as in the Red Indian mythology): that of an almost pantheistic force or power which incarnates itself in the phenomena of the actual world and of which

by cold and heat without representing the elements earth and fire, whereas the West corresponds at the same time both to moisture and to water; the East represents dryness and above all light, but not air. This asymmetry can be explained as follows: the elements air and earth are respectively identified, in the spatial symbolism of the Universe, with Heaven and Earth, hence with the extremities of the vertical axis, whereas fire—to the extent it is sacrificial and transmuting—is the Center of all things; if one takes account of the fact that Heaven synthesizes all the active aspects of both quaternaries—that of the elements[11] and that of the states[12]—and that Earth synthesizes their passive aspects, it will be seen that the symbolical definitions of the four quarters are intended as a synthesis of the two poles, the one heavenly and the other earthly:[13] the Axis North-South is earthly, and the Axis East-West is heavenly.

What is common to all the American Indians is the fourfold polarity of cosmic qualities, but the descriptive symbolism can vary from one group to another, especially between groups differing as much as the Sioux and the Iroquois. Among the Cherokees, for instance, who belong to the Iroquois family, East, South, West, North mean respectively success, happiness, death, adversity and are represented by the colors, red, white, black, blue; for the Sioux all the cardinal points have a positive meaning, their colors being—in the same order of succession—red, yellow, black, white; but there is evidently a relationship between North-adversity and North-purification since trials purify and strengthen, or between West-death and West-revelation, since both ideas are related to the hereafter. Among the Ojibway, who belong to the Algonquin group, East is white like light, South green like vegetation, West red or yellow like the setting sun, and North black like the night; the attributions differ with the different points of view, but the fundamental symbolism with its fourfold structure and polarities is not affected.

*   *   *

this world is but an image or illusion" (*L'art et la philosophie des Indiens de l'Amérique du Nord* [Paris, 1926]).

[11] Air, fire, water, earth.

[12] Dryness, warmth, moisture, cold.

[13] This means—if one considers all this symbolism in the light of alchemy—that in the polarization in question the complementary forces of the "sulfur", which "dilates", and the "mercury", which "contracts" and "dissolves", are in equilib-

The crucial part played by the directions of space in the rite of the Calumet or Sacred Pipe is well known. This rite is the Indian's prayer, in which he speaks not only on his own behalf but also on behalf of all other creatures; the entire Universe prays together with the man who offers the Pipe to the Powers or Power.

Let us also mention here the other great rites of American Indian Shamanism, at least the principal ones, namely, the Sweat Lodge, solitary Invocation, and the Sun Dance;[14] we choose the number four not because it marks any absolute limit, but because it is sacred to the Indians and because it allows of establishing a synthesis that has nothing arbitrary about it.

The Sweat Lodge is a purificatory rite without peer; man is cleansed by it and becomes a new being. This rite and that of the Pipe are absolutely fundamental; the one that follows is so as well, but in a somewhat different sense.

Solitary Invocation—"lamenting" or "sending forth a voice"—is the most exalted form of prayer; it can be silent,[15] as circumstances dictate. It is a true spiritual retreat, through which every Indian has to pass once in his youth—the intention then is a special one—and which he may repeat periodically according to inspiration or circumstances.

The Sun Dance is in a sense the prayer of the whole community; for those who participate, it means—esoterically at least—a virtual union with the solar Spirit, hence with the Great Spirit. This Dance symbolizes the connection of the soul to the Divinity: just as the dancer is connected to the central tree—by thongs that symbolize the rays of the sun—so man is connected to Heaven by a mysterious bond, which at one time the Indian sealed with his own blood, whereas now he is satisfied to keep uninterrupted fast for three or four days.* The dancer in this rite is like an eagle flying toward the sun: with a whistle made from the bone of an eagle, he produces a shrill and plaintive sound while imitating in a certain fashion the eagle's flight by using feathers he carries in his hands. This as it were

---

rium; the central fire is then equivalent to the Hermetic fire at the bottom of the athanor.

[14] Other rites are more social in their scope.

[15] *Cf.* René Guénon, "Silence et Solitude", *Études Traditionnelles* (March, 1949).

* Translator's note: Over a period of many years, government policies had resulted in the practice of "piercing" at the Sun Dance being largely suppressed, but this

sacramental relationship with the sun leaves an ineffaceable mark on the soul.[16]

*   *   *

Regarding the magical practices of shamans, it is necessary to distinguish ordinary magic from what might be called cosmic magic; the cosmic type operates by virtue of the analogies between symbols and their prototypes. Everywhere in nature, which includes man himself, we discover in fact similar possibilities: substances, forms, and movements that correspond to one another qualitatively or typologically; now the shaman aims at mastering phenomena that lie outside his control, whether by their nature or by accident, through the use of other phenomena of an analogous—and therefore metaphysically "identical"—kind, which he himself creates and which are thereby brought within his own sphere of activity; he may wish to bring rain, stop a snow-storm, cause the arrival of a herd of bison, or cure an illness, and for this purpose he makes use of forms, colors, rhythms, incantations, and wordless melodies. All this would be insufficient, however, were it not for the shaman's extraordinary power of concentration, which is acquired through a long training carried out in solitude and silence and in contact with virgin nature;[17] concentration can also be the result of an exceptional gift or may come through the intervention of a celestial influence.[18] Behind every sensible phenomenon there lies a reality of an animistic order, which is independent of the limitations of space and time; it is by placing himself in contact with these realities or these subtle and supra-sensorial roots of things that a shaman is able to influence natural phenomena or foretell the future. All this may seem strange—to say the least—to a modern reader, whose imagina-

---

is now no longer the case. Nonetheless, not all the tribes that practiced piercing during the pre-reservation era include it in the Sun Dance today.

[16] All these rites have been described by Hehaka Sapa in *The Sacred Pipe* by Joseph E. Brown (University of Oklahoma Press, 1953). His Holiness the Jagadguru of Kanchipuram, having read this book, remarked to one of our friends that the Red Indian rites share striking analogies with certain Vedic rites. [Translator's note: the most recent edition is *The Sacred Pipe* (Norman: University of Oklahoma, 1989).]

[17] Ever since medicine-men have lived in houses—a Shoshone told us—they have become impure and lost much of their power.

[18] As in the case of Hehaka Sapa.

tion now bears different imprints and obeys different reflexes than did that of mediaeval or archaic man and whose subconscious, it must be said, is therefore warped by a mass of prejudices having intellectual or scientific pretensions; without going into details, let us simply recall with Shakespeare that "there are more things in heaven and earth than are dreamt of in your philosophy".

But shamans are also, and even *a fortiori*, expert magicians in the ordinary sense; their science works with forces of a psychic or animistic order, whether individualized or otherwise; unlike cosmic magic, it does not introduce analogies between the microcosm and the macrocosm or between the various natural reverberations of the same "idea". In "white magic", which is normally the kind used by shamans, the forces set into motion as well as the purpose of the operation are either beneficent or simply neutral; when on the contrary the spirits are malefic and the purpose equally so, "black magic" or sorcery is involved; in this case nothing is done "in the name of God", and the link with the higher powers is broken. It goes without saying that practices so socially dangerous or so pernicious in themselves were strictly prohibited among the American Indians as among all peoples,[19] though this does not mean these practices did not undergo in the case of certain forest tribes a spread of almost epidemic proportions—just as in Europe at the end of the Middle Ages—in conformity with their sinister and contagious nature.

One problem that has preoccupied all who take an interest in the spirituality of the American Indians is that of the "Dance of the Spirits" (the Ghost Dance), which played so tragic a part in their final defeat. Contrary to current opinion, this dance was not an entirely unprecedented occurrence; several similar movements had arisen long before Wovoka, the originator of the Ghost Dance. In fact the following phenomenon occurred fairly often among the tribes of the West: a visionary, who was not necessarily a shaman, underwent an experience of death and, upon returning to life, brought a message from the hereafter that took the form of prophecies concerning the end of the world, the return of the dead, and the creation of a new earth—some even spoke of a "rain of stars"—then a call to peace and finally a dance designed to hasten

---

[19] Except perhaps among some very degenerate Melanesian tribes.

these events and protect the faithful, in this case the Indians; in a word, these messages from beyond the grave contained eschatological and "millenarian" conceptions, which we meet in one form or another in all mythologies and religions.[20]

What made the story of the Ghost Dance so distinctive and tragic were the physical and psychological conditions prevailing at that moment: the despair of the Indians transposed these prophecies into the immediate future and conferred on them in addition a combative tone quite out of keeping with the peaceful character of the original message; nonetheless it was not the Indians who provoked the conflict. As for the prodigies experienced by certain believers—especially among the Sioux—they seem to have been not so much phenomena of suggestion as hallucinations resulting from a collective psychosis as well as being determined in part by Christian influences; Wovoka always denied having claimed to be Christ, whereas he never denied having encountered the divine Being—which can be understood in many different ways—nor having received a message; and yet he had no motive for denying the first rather than the second.[21] It seems to us there is no reason to accuse Wovoka of imposture, especially since he has been described as a man of sincerity by Whites who at least had no prejudice in his favor; doubtless the truth is that he too was a victim of circumstances. To see this whole movement in its proper proportions one must consider it within its traditional context—taking into account Indian "polyprophetism" as well as the "apocalypticism" common to all religions—and at the same time within its contingent and temporal context, namely, the collapse of the vital foundations of the Plains civilization.

*   *   *

---

[20] Certain completely analogous movements occurred successively in Peru and Bolivia from the time of the Spanish Conquest to the beginning of the twentieth century.

[21] *Cf.* James Mooney, "The Ghost-Dance Religion", in the *Fourteenth Annual Report of the Bureau of Ethnology to the Secretary of the Smithsonian Institution* (Washington, 1896); also Leslie Spier, "The Prophet Dance of the North-West", in *General Series in Anthropology* (Menasha, Wisconsin, 1935).

A fascinating combination of combative and stoical heroism with a priestly bearing conferred on the Indian of the Plains and Forests a sort of majesty at once aquiline and solar, hence the powerfully original and irreplaceable beauty which is associated with him and which contributes to his prestige as a warrior and martyr.[22] Like the Japanese at the time of the Samurai, the Indian was in the deepest sense an artist when it came to the manifestation of his personality: apart from the fact that his life was a ceaseless sporting with suffering and death,[23] and thus a kind of chivalrous *karma yoga*,[24] he knew how to impart to this spiritual style an aesthetic adornment unsurpassable in its expressiveness.

One factor which may have given the impression that the Indian is an individualist—in principle and not merely *de facto*—is the crucial importance he attaches to the moral worth of a man, to character one might say, and hence to the cult of action.[25] The heroic and silent act is contrasted with the empty and prolix speech of the coward; love of secrecy, a reluctance to express what is sacred by means of glib speeches that weaken and disperse it, can be explained in this way. The whole Indian character can be summed up in two words, if such an ellipsis may be permitted: act and secret—the act, shattering if need be, and the secret implacable. Rock-like, the Indian of former times reposed in himself, in his personality, ready to translate it into action with the impetuosity of lightning; but at the same time he remained humble before

---

[22] Whatever anti-romantic pseudo-realists, who believe in nothing but the trivial, may think. If no so-called primitive people has aroused an interest as lively and lasting as have the Indians, and if they embody some of our nostalgias often wrongly described as puerile, it really must be that they are something in themselves, for "there is no smoke without fire".

[23] An "ordeal", as Hartley Burr Alexander described it.

[24] Black Elk's son told us that among the Indian warriors there were some who vowed to die on the battlefield; they were called "those who do not return", and they carried special insignia, notably a staff adorned with feathers and a curved point. We have also heard this from the Crow Indians.

[25] "What can never be taken away from a man," one Sioux told us, "is his education; one cannot remove it or buy it. Each man must form his own character and personality; one who is content to let himself go will fall, and he will bear the responsibility." No less typical is the following thought as expressed by the same man: "When an Indian smokes the Pipe, he directs it toward the four quarters and toward Heaven and earth, and after that he must watch his tongue, his actions, and his character."

the Great Mystery, whose permanent message, he knew, lay in the nature all around him.

Nature is linked with holy poverty as with spiritual childlikeness; it is an open book containing an inexhaustible teaching of truth and beauty. It is in the midst of his own artifices that man most easily becomes corrupted, for it is they that make him greedy and impious; close to virgin nature, which knows neither agitation nor falsehood, man has the chance of remaining contemplative like nature herself. And it is nature—total and quasi-divine, and beyond all human waywardness—which will have the final word.

*   *   *

In order to understand fully the sudden fate of the Indian race, it is necessary to take account of the fact that this race had lived for thousands of years in a kind of paradise that was practically without limits; the Indians of the West were still living under such conditions at the beginning of the nineteenth century. Theirs was a rugged paradise, to be sure, but one that nevertheless provided an environment full of grandeur and at the same time sacred, comparable in many respects with the northern parts of Europe before the coming of the Romans.[26] Since the Indians identified themselves spiritually and humanly with this inviolate—and in their view inviolable—nature, they accepted all her laws and therefore also the struggle for life inasmuch as it was a manifestation of "the principle of the best"; but with the passage of time and the growing effects of the "Iron Age", in which passions predominate and wisdom disappears, abuses began to spread more and more; a heroic, but vindictive and cruel, individualism obscured the disinterested virtues, as indeed happened to all other warrior peoples. The privileged situation of the Indians—outside the pale of "History" and its crushing urban civilizations—inevitably had to come to an end; there is nothing surprising in the fact that this disintegration of a paradise, which had in a certain sense grown old, coincided with modern times.[27]

[26] The Germans lived in hamlets and the Gauls in towns, but all their buildings were of wood, and this fact marks a fundamental difference between them and the Mediterranean people, who lived in stone-built cities.

[27] Last Bull—formerly custodian of the sacred arrows of the Cheyenne—told us about an ancient prophecy of his tribe: a man would come from the East holding

Nevertheless it is abundantly clear that to speak of fatality alone is one-sided and cannot extenuate or excuse the villainies of which the Indian has been a victim for several centuries, unless notions of justice and injustice are meaningless and there have never been such things as infamy or tragedy. Apologists for the white invasion and its consequences are only too ready to argue that all peoples in all ages have committed acts of violence; violence, yes, but not necessarily acts of baseness, perpetrated moreover in the name of liberty, equality, fraternity, civilization, progress, and the rights of man. The conscious, calculated, methodical, official, and by no means anonymous destruction of the red race, its traditions and culture, in North America and partially also in South America, far from having been an unavoidable process—and as such possibly excusable in the name of natural laws, provided one does not claim to have outgrown those laws thanks to "civilization"—certainly remains one of the greatest crimes and most notorious vandalisms of all time.

This said, there remains the ineluctable aspect of things, the aspect of fatality, by virtue of which what is possible cannot but be manifested in some manner or other, and according to which everything that happens has its causes, whether proximate or distant; this aspect of the world and destiny does not prevent things, however, from being what they are; evil remains evil at its own level. Evil is to be condemned for its nature, not for its inevitability; this inevitability must be accepted, for tragedy necessarily enters into the divine play, if only because the world is not God; one must not accept error, but one must be resigned to its existence. But beyond earthly destructions there is the Indestructible: "Every form you see," sings Rumi, "has its archetype in the divine world, beyond space; if the form perishes, what matter is that, since its heavenly model is indestructible? Every beautiful form you have seen, every meaningful word you have heard—be not sorrowful that all this must be lost; for it is not really so. The divine Source is immortal, and its spring gives water unceasingly; since neither the one nor the other can be stopped, wherefore do you lament? From the first moment when you entered this world of existence, a ladder has been set up before you."

---

a leaf or skin covered with graphic signs; he would show this leaf and declare that it had come from the Creator of the world; and he would destroy men, trees, and grasses in order to replace them with other men, other trees, other grasses.

Tracing *Mâyâ*

Mâyâ is not only "universal illusion", but also "divine play". It is the great theophany, the "unveiling" of God[1] "in Himself and by Himself", as the Sufis would say.[2] *Mâyâ* is like a magic fabric woven from a warp that veils and a weft that unveils; a quasi-incomprehensible intermediary between the finite and the Infinite—at least from our point of view as creatures[3]—it has all the shimmering ambiguity appropriate to its half-cosmic, half-divine nature.

The doctrine of the Vedantists is incontestably metaphysical in the highest possible sense; it transmits every essential truth, although it is possible that the doctrine of the Sufis is more explicit on one point, namely, the "why" or "how" of the projection of the "divine play". Hindus readily declare that *Mâyâ* is inexplicable; Muslims on the contrary insist on the "divine purpose" of creation in keeping with the saying: "I was a hidden treasure, I desired to be known,[4] and thus I created the world":[5] the world is a "dimension" of the infinity of God, if one may so express it. In other words, if Allah did not possess the quality of "outwardness" (*az-Zâhir*), among others, He would not be God; or again, He alone has the capacity to introduce reality into nothingness.[6] It is true that the divine qualities which are opposites—such as "outwardness" and "inwardness", "justice" and "mercy", "forgiveness" and "vengeance"[7]—are

---

[1] In the three Semitic monotheisms, the name "God" necessarily embraces all that belongs to the Principle with no restriction whatever, although the exoterisms obviously consider the ontological aspect alone.

[2] There are various expressions of this kind. According to the *Risâlat al-Ahadîyah*, "He sent His ipseity by Himself from Himself to Himself."

[3] For in reality nothing is outside the Infinite.

[4] Or "I desired to know", that is, in distinctive mode and in relativity.

[5] *Hadîth qudsî.*

[6] Such a mode of expression may seem logically absurd, but its intellectual function and metaphysical import—analogous to the no less contradictory idea of the geometrical point—will not escape those familiar with our works.

[7] But not the simple or non-complementary qualities, such as "unity", "holiness", "wisdom", "beatitude". These qualities belong to the Essence, and it is our manner of dissociating them—and not their intrinsic nature—that pertains to *Mâyâ*. "Wisdom" is in "holiness" and conversely, whereas opposed qualities such as "rigor" and "clemency" are irreducible and irreversible.

themselves already within the domain of *Mâyâ* or there would be no opposition between them, and yet each expresses a mystery of the Essence or supreme Self; for all divine aspects, extrinsic as well as intrinsic, are linked together by virtue of the unity of the Essence.

If the world is necessary by virtue of a mystery of the divine infinity—and there must be no confusing the perfection of necessity with constraint nor the perfection of liberty with arbitrariness—the necessity of creative Being must come before that of the world, and with all the more reason: what the world is to Being, Being is—*mutatis mutandis*—to supreme Non-Being. Not only does *Mâyâ* encompass manifestation; it is affirmed already *a fortiori* "within" the Principle; the divine Principle, "desiring to be known"—or "desiring to know"—condescends to the unfolding of its inward infinity, an unfolding at first potential and then outward or cosmic.[8] The relationship "God-world", "Creator-creature", "Principle-manifestation" would be inconceivable if it were not prefigured in God, independently of any question of creation.

To say that *Mâyâ* is "inexplicable" does not mean that there is an insoluble problem; the only unanswerable question is the "why" of the supreme Principle, of *Âtmâ*, and it is insoluble because it is absurd, since the Absolute cannot be explained by anything relative; the Absolute is either incomprehensible or dazzlingly obvious. On the other hand, the question of the "why" of *Mâyâ* is not meaningless, provided however that one has in view pure causality and not some kind of anthropomorphic motivation; relativity has its sufficient reason in the Absolute and is therefore evident by reference to the Absolute, while remaining problematic in itself. We can understand why the Absolute necessarily engenders the relative, but there is something in the relative that eludes our need for explanations, namely, the "why" of this or that chance event; we understand the theory of possibilities, but the choice, the arrangement, the coincidences of what is possible remain mysterious to us; things are obscure inasmuch as they belong to relativity, and if there could be such a thing as pure relativity, it would be pure obscurity and unintelligibility. But our very incomprehension is here a sort of comprehension: if we do not understand, it is because there is necessarily

---

[8] In Christian language—we do not say "theological" language—one could say that the Father caused Himself to be engendered as Son in order that the Son might be able to make himself man, or in order that God might make Himself world.

in the Universe a margin for the gratuitous and inexplicable, which in its way manifests divine liberty. Or again, if we start from the idea that the Absolute—and the Absolute alone—is perfectly intelligible and unconditionally evident, we may conclude as a corollary that the relative is unintelligible, equivocal, doubtful; this is the viewpoint of Vedantists. *Mâyâ* is none other than relativity, which in certain respects is more "mysterious" than the Absolute; but "mystery" then signifies something indirect, negative, and chaotic. In short, Hindus insist on this aspect of arbitrariness and indefiniteness precisely to the extent that they fix their gaze upon the "superabundance of clarity"—as Saint Thomas would say—of pure Reality.

It is to a great extent from this unintelligible—and in a sense "absurd"—aspect of *Mâyâ* or *Prakriti*[9] that there arises this disturbing element which insinuates itself into our mental crystallizations as soon as they depart from their normal function, which is indicative and not exhaustive; to speak of an absolute adequation of our thought to the Real is a contradiction in terms since our thought is not the Real and since the meaning of this equation is precisely this separation or difference. To conclude that total truth is inaccessible to us is an even greater error, one linked moreover to the preceding error through a confusion between direct knowledge and thought; if the fact that we can have a perfectly adequate notion of a tree does not mean that our thought is identified with the tree, the contrary fact that our adequation is not an identity does not mean that we are unable to know the tree in any way. Be that as it may, the desire to enclose universal Reality within an exclusive and exhaustive "explanation" brings with it a permanent disequilibrium because of the interferences of *Mâyâ*, and it is moreover just this disequilibrium and restlessness that are the life of modern philosophy; but this aspect of unintelligibility or "irrationality" in *Mâyâ*—this enigmatic and almost "mocking" element that condemns philosophy "according to the flesh" (Saint Paul) to a vicious circle and finally to suicide—results in the final analysis from the transcendence of the Principle, which will no more allow itself to be imprisoned by blind ratiocinations than will our sensory faculties allow themselves to be

---

[9] We are not saying that these two ideas are synonymous; our juxtaposition signifies that *Prakriti*, the ontological "Substance", is the divine "femininity" of *Mâyâ*. The "masculine" aspect is represented by the divine Names, which—insofar as they correspond to *Purusha*—determine and "fertilize" Substance in collaboration with the three fundamental tendencies included within it (the *gunas*: *sattva, rajas, tamas*).

perceived by our senses; we say "imprisoned", for the "indicative" value of well-founded logical operations is not in question.

What permits us to speak about an aspect of "absurdity" in *Mâyâ* is that there is something inevitably contradictory in relativity, as is shown for example by the plurality of the ego—logically unique though it is—or by the unimaginable but undeniable limitlessness of space, time, number, diversity, matter. In comparison with the always precarious perfections of the world, the divine Person certainly possesses supereminently all the perfections of which the world offers us traces, but from the point of view of His supra-ontological Essence it is impossible to assert that the ontological restriction possesses the perfection of pure absoluteness[10] or that the opposition between certain divine Names contains no kind of contradiction; nonetheless it is impossible to speak of "absurdity" outside manifestation, hence in what pertains to the creating God as such and as distinguished from the supreme Divinity by the effect of *Mâyâ*, which comes into play at this point. It should be added that the opposition of the divine Names disappears in their ineffable roots: at the level of Being there is indeed opposition between "forgiveness" and "vengeance", but above that level these two Names are united in their common Essence; there is a "dilation" so to speak, but not an "abolition".

We mentioned the "creating God" with the addition of the words "as such": this precautionary qualification is far from superfluous, for to speak of "Being"—unless a distinctive definition is intended—is to speak of "Non-Being" or "Beyond-Being"; crucially important shades of meaning are to be noted here, for one cannot speak of God in just any way. Being, defined as such, is not Beyond-Being or the supreme Self; but "God" is always "God"—where there is no express metaphysical reservation—and this means that there are aspects in Him but not compartments and that these aspects always remain inseparable from Divinity as a whole.

The distinction in God between a trans-ontological and transpersonal Essence, on the one hand, and an already relative "auto-determination", which is Being or the Person,[11] on the other hand, marks

---

[10] The adjective "pure" does not constitute a pleonasm in this case, since the idea of the "relatively absolute" is for us of the highest metaphysical or even simply logical importance.

[11] One finds in the works of Meister Eckhart, Silesius, Omar Khayyam, and others expressions which seem to make the "existence" of God depend on that of man, but

the whole difference between the strictly metaphysical or sapiential perspective and cataphatic and ontologistic theologies insofar as they are explicit. Let us remember here that the Intellect—which is precisely what makes evident to us the absoluteness of the Self and the relativity of "objectifications"—is "human" only to the extent that it is accessible to us, but not in itself; it is essentially *increatus et increabile* (Eckhart), although "accidentally" created by virtue of its reverberations in the macrocosm and in microcosms; geometrically speaking, the Intellect is a ray rather than a circle: it "emanates" from God before "reflecting" Him. "Allah is known to Himself alone," say the Sufis; while this saying apparently excludes man from direct and total knowledge, it actually expresses the essential and mysterious divinity of the pure Intellect; formulas of this kind are fully understandable only in light of the often quoted *hadîth*: "Whoso knoweth his soul knoweth his Lord."

The sun, not being God, must prostrate itself every evening before the throne of Allah; thus it is said in Islam. Similarly *Mâyâ*, not being *Âtmâ*, can affirm itself only intermittently; the worlds spring from the divine Word and return into it. Instability is the price of contingency; to ask why there will be an end of the world and a resurrection amounts to asking why a respiratory phase stops at a precise moment to be followed by the opposite phase, or why a wave withdraws from the shore after submerging it, or again why the drops of a fountain fall back to earth. We are divine possibilities projected into the night of existence and diversified by reason of that very projection, as water is scattered into drops when it is launched into space and is crystallized when seized by cold.

To speak of "manifestation" is to speak of "reintegration"; the error of materialists—or their lack of imagination, if one prefers—is to take matter as an unvarying given[12] whereas it is only a movement that our experience of ephemera cannot encompass—a kind of transitory contraction of a substance that is in itself inaccessible to our senses; it is as if we noticed only the solidity of ice without knowing that ice had ever been water or that the water had ever been a cloud. Our empirical matter, with all it comprises, is derived

---

which mean in fact that the Intellect penetrates into the "depths of God" and hence that it can surpass the level of reality of the ontological Principle.

[12] Regardless of the subtleties with which one presumes to "surpass" the idea of matter and which merely displace the idea without changing its level.

from a supra-sensible and eminently plastic proto-matter, which is determined by the "creative Breath";[13] in this proto-matter earthly being was reflected and "incarnated", something that the myth of the sacrifice of *Purusha* expresses in its own way. Under the segmenting effect of this proto-matter, the divine image became diversified; but creatures were still "states of consciousness", contemplative states turned toward the inward and illumined in themselves, and it is in this sense that it could be said that in Paradise sheep and wolves live side by side. It is in this proto-material *hylê* that the creation of species took place; after the bipolarization of the primordial androgyne came its "exteriorization", namely, the "fall of Adam", which in turn—since within this subtle and luminous proto-matter everything was as it were conjoined—brought in its wake the "materialization" of all earthly creatures, hence their "crystallization" and the oppositions that necessarily resulted from it. Conflicts and calamities cannot but exist in a material world, and to seek to abolish them—instead of choosing the lesser evil—is the most pernicious of illusions.

Man is like a reduced image of the cosmogonic unfolding: we are made of matter, but in the center of our being is the supra-sensible and transcendent, the "kingdom of Heaven", the "eye of the heart", the passageway to the Infinite. To suppose that matter—which in reality is but an instant—is "at the beginning" of the Universe amounts to asserting that flesh can produce intelligence or that stone can produce flesh. If God is the "omega", He is also the "alpha": the Word is "in the beginning" and not "at the end" alone, as would suit the purposes of a pseudo-religious evolutionism, the metaphysical nullity of which is self-evident. "Emanation" is strictly discontinuous because of the transcendence and immutability of the divine Substance, for any continuity would affect the Creator as a result of creation, *quod absit*. There is a theory—but God knows best—according to which the stellar universe is an immense explosion proceeding from an imperceptible nucleus; whatever the value of this conception, the total Universe—of which the visible universe is only a tiny cell—could be described in the same way, provided that the image is not taken literally; what we mean to say is that the

---

[13] We are recapitulating a short description already provided in the chapter "Fall and Forfeiture", one that is of paramount importance.

manifestation of *Mâyâ*,[14] which in its totality obviously eludes our sensory faculties and imagination, follows an analogous and therefore centrifugal movement until the possibilities that were lent it by Being are exhausted; sooner or later every expansion attains a point of ultimate depletion, its "end of the world" or "last Judgment".

Some people have reached the conclusion that space is spherical, but their principles and methods cut them off from access to a truth which is nonetheless fundamental and without which all speculation on the destiny of the world and of things remains vain, namely, that time is no less circular, as indeed is everything that pertains to *Mâyâ*. An Indian, speaking of the "Great Spirit", has very rightly called attention to the fact that "everything the Power of the World does is done in a circle. The sky is round. . . . Even the seasons form a great circle in their changing, and they always come back again to where they were."[15] Thus all that exists proceeds by way of gyratory movements, everything springing from the Absolute and returning to the Absolute;[16] it is because the relative cannot be conceived otherwise than as a "circular emergence" from the Absolute—an emergence that is therefore transitory inasmuch as it returns to its source—that space is round and that creatures encounter at the end of their lives the nothingness from which they emerged, and then the Absolute that has lent them their existence. To say that man is relative—which is a pleonasm since he exists— amounts to saying that he will inexorably encounter the Absolute; relativity is a circle and the first of all circles; *Mâyâ* can be described symbolically as a great circular movement and also as a spherical state.[17] Death cannot destroy the ego or else it would be possible to annihilate the spirit by material means, hence to create it by material means as well—a senseless hypothesis since the "lesser" has no absolute power over the "greater" outside the quantitative domain.

---

[14] *Mâyâ* non-manifested, as we have said, is Being, *Îshvara*.

[15] Black Elk (Hehaka Sapa) in *Black Elk Speaks* (New York, 1932, reprinted University of Nebraska Press, Lincoln, U.S.A., 1961).

[16] One must always take account of the difference between the "relative Absolute", which is creative Being, and the "pure Absolute", which is Non-Being, the Essence, the Self; therein lies the difference between the "end of the world" and the *apocatastasis* or between the *pralaya* and the *mahâpralaya*.

[17] This corresponds exactly to the Buddhist diagrams of the "round of existence" or the "wheel of things". *Samsâra* is at the same time a circle and a rotation.

According to the degree of its conformity to its Origin, the creature will be retained or rejected by the Creator; and Existence in its totality will finally return, with Being itself, into the infinity of the Self. *Mâyâ* returns to *Âtmâ*, although strictly speaking nothing can depart from *Âtmâ* nor therefore return to it.

The mission of man is to introduce the Absolute into the relative, if one may use so elliptical an expression; since man has all too often failed in his mission, this is also therefore the role of Revelation and the *Avatâra* as well as of miracles. In a miracle as in other theophanies, the veil of *Mâyâ* is symbolically torn; the miracle, the Prophet, wisdom are metaphysically necessary, for it is inconceivable that they should not appear within the world of man; and man himself comprises all these aspects in relationship to the terrestrial world, of which he is the center and opening toward Heaven, or *pontifex*. The meaning of human life—to paraphrase a Christian formula expressing the reciprocity between man and God—is to realize that *Âtmâ* became *Mâyâ* that *Mâyâ* might become *Âtmâ*.[18]

[18] It is in an analogous sense that the Buddhists say that *Shûnya* (the "Void", the world) is *Nirvâna* ("Extinction", the Absolute) and that *Nirvâna* is *Shûnya*.

Naiveté

Attributing a naive outlook to everyone who lived in the past is the simplest way of exalting oneself, and it is all the easier and more tempting because it is founded in part on accurate though fragmentary observations, which can be made the most of—with the help of mistaken generalizations and arbitrary interpretations—when linked to a progressivist evolutionism. It is necessary first of all to come to some agreement as to what naiveté means. If to be naive is to be direct and spontaneous, to know nothing of dissimulation and subterfuge and doubtless also nothing of certain experiences, then unmodernized peoples certainly possess—or possessed—that kind of naiveté; but if it is merely to be without intelligence or critical sense and to be open to all kinds of deception, then there is certainly no reason to suppose that our contemporaries are any less naive than our ancestors.

However that may be, there are few things that the "insulated" being who calls himself "a man of our times" endures less readily than the risk of appearing naive; everything else can go by the board so long as the feeling of not being duped by anything is safeguarded. In reality the acme of naiveté is to believe that man can escape from naiveté on every plane and that it is possible for him to be integrally intelligent by his own efforts; whoever seeks to gain all things by cleverness ends by losing all in blindness and ineffectuality. Those who reproach our ancestors with having been stupidly credulous forget in the first place that one can also be stupidly incredulous, and in the second place that the self-styled destroyers of illusion live on illusions that exemplify a credulity second to none; for a simple credulity can be replaced by a complicated one, adorned with the arabesques of a studied doubt that forms part of the style, but it is still credulity: complication does not make error less false, nor stupidity less stupid.

Contrary to the popular image of a hopelessly naive Middle Ages and a breathtakingly intelligent twentieth century must be set the fact that history does not abolish simplicity of outlook, but merely displaces it, together with the fact that the most flagrant form of naiveté is to fail to see naiveté where it exists; moreover there is nothing more simplistic than a pretension to "begin from scratch" on every plane, nor than the systematic—and unbelievably insolent—self-uprooting that characterizes certain tendencies of the contemporary world. It is fashionable to regard not only the people of the Middle Ages but even those of fairly recent generations as having been duped in every possible way, so that to resemble them would be a matter for shame; in this respect the nineteenth century seems almost as remote as the Merovingian age. Opinions now current prove that people think themselves incomparably more "realistic" than anyone has ever been, even in the recent past; "our time" or "the twentieth century" or "the atomic age" seems to hover, like an uprooted island or a fabulously "clearheaded" monad, above millennia of childishness and blundering. The contemporary world is like a man ashamed of having had parents and wanting to create himself, and to recreate space, time, and all the physical laws, or seeking to extract from nothingness a world objectively perfect and subjectively comfortable, and all this by means of a creative activity independent of God or opposed to God; the unfortunate thing is that attempts to create a new order of Being can only end in self-destruction.

The average young person of today tends, it seems, to hold our fathers responsible for all ills; that is a completely absurd atti-tude, for not only could our fathers reproach their fathers in the same way, and so on for ever, but there is also nothing to prove that children of the present-day youth will not one day have solid reasons to level the same reproach at their elders. If these young people make themselves out to be innocent in principle because they have no ideology and are not interested in politics, they forget that a world can go adrift precisely for that reason; a misfortune can come about because someone does something, but it can also come about because no one does anything, all the more so in that no one is alone in the world and others take on the job of thinking and acting for those who wish to do neither. Contemporary man has collected a great mass of experiences and is therefore rather disillusioned, but the conclusions he draws from it are so false that they virtually reduce to nothing all that has been gained, or ought to have been gained.

*   *   *

A fact that can lead to error, and one that is not left unexploited, is the analogy between the childhood of individuals and that of peoples; the analogy is only partial, however, and in a certain respect it is even inverse, the collectivity being in this respect the opposite—or the inverted image—of the individual. In fact, whereas in individuals it is age that normally represents wisdom, in a traditional collectivity, as well as in humanity considered as a whole, wisdom coincides with the origin, that is to say, with the "apostolic period" in a civilization and with the "golden age" in humanity as a whole; but just as every civilization declines, like humanity itself, as it gets farther from its origins and nearer to the "end times", so does the individual decline, at least physically, with age; and just as the period of Revelation or the "golden age" is a time when Heaven and earth are in contact and when Angels speak with men, so the childhood of the individual is in some respects a time of innocence, of happiness, and of nearness to Heaven; there is therefore a direct analogy between individual life and the cycles of the collectivity, and this is in parallel with an inverse analogy that situates wisdom at the origin of the life of the collectivity and at the end of the life of the individual. Nevertheless, it is undeniable that an old society has gathered experiences and developed arts—though this is merely an outward expression—and it is precisely this fact that leads to error when the postulates of evolutionism are accepted *a priori*.

There is clearly an important distinction between a naiveté that is intrinsic and one that is extrinsic; an extrinsic naiveté exists only accidentally and in relation to a world that is the product of certain experiences, but it is full of hypocrisy, useless cleverness, and dissimulation; how could a man who is unaware of the existence of falsehood, or who knows it only as a deadly and exceptional sin, appear as otherwise than ingenuous to a mean-spirited and artful society? To a pathologically crafty person every normal man seems naive; for the swindlers it is the honest fellows who are artless. Even where a certain critical sense exists, it is far from constituting a superiority in itself, being merely an excrescence produced by an environment in which everything is falsified: it is thus that nature produces self-defensive reflexes and adaptations that can be explained only by a particular environment or prevailing circumstances; there is no difficulty in admitting that the physical particularities of an Eskimo or Bushman do not in themselves constitute a superiority.

If the men of old sometimes appear ingenuous, it is often because they are considered from a distorted point of view, which is the result of a more or less generalized corruption; to accuse them of being naive amounts to applying a law to them retroactively, to express ourselves in legal terms. Likewise, if an ancient writer can give the impression of simplemindedness, this is largely because he did not have to take account of a thousand errors still unknown nor of a thousand possibilities of misinterpretation, and also because there was no need for his dialectic to be like the Scottish dance between the eggs, seeing that such an author could in a large measure dispense with nuances; words still possessed a freshness and a fullness—or a magic—which it is difficult for us to imagine, living as we do in a climate of verbal inflation.

Naiveté occurring merely from a lack of experience is of course a purely relative affair: men in general, and collectivities in any case, cannot help being unsophisticated about experiences which they have not had and which concern possibilities they are not able to foresee, and it is easy for those who have had such experiences to judge the inexperience of others and believe themselves superior; the worth of men is not decided by their accumulation of experience, but by their capacity to profit from it. We may be more perspicacious than others with regard to what we have experienced, but at the same time more naive than they with regard to what we have yet to experience—or what we are incapable of experiencing, while others may have done so in our place; for it is one thing to have lived through an event and another to have drawn the right conclusions from it. Playing with fire because one does not know that it burns is no doubt a kind of naiveté, but jumping into a river because one has burnt a finger is certainly no better, for to be unaware that fire burns is no more naive than to be unaware that one can escape from fire otherwise than by drowning. The great, the classic, error is that of curing abuses by other abuses—apparently of less significance but really more fundamental inasmuch as they compromise principles; in other words it is the error of getting rid of the disease by killing the patient.

*　　*　　*

There is a kind of naiveté with which our ancestors could be reproached on the plane of the physical sciences and which takes the form of a certain confusion between domains: because of a lack of experience or observation—although in itself this is certainly nothing to worry about—they were sometimes inclined to overestimate the scope of cosmic correspondences; for this reason they tended imprudently to apply to one order laws applicable to another and hence to believe, for instance, that salamanders can resist fire, and even put it out, owing to certain properties of these batrachians and even more to a confusion between them and the "fiery spirits" of the same name; the men of old were all the more liable to such mistakes because they still knew from experience the protean character of the subtle substance that envelops and penetrates the material world—in other words, because the barrier between the corporeal and psychic states was less solidified than in later periods. In return, the men of today are themselves relatively excusable on this same plane, but in a contrary sense, in that their total lack of experience of perceptible psychic manifestations seems to confirm them in their materialism; nonetheless, whatever the inexperience of modern man in things belonging to the psychic or subtle order, there are still phenomena of this kind, which are by no means inaccessible to him in principle, but he labels them *a priori* as "superstitions" and abandons them to occultists.

Acceptance of the psychic dimension is in any case a part of religion: one cannot deny magic without straying from faith; so far as miracles are concerned, their cause surpasses the psychic plane, though their effects come by way of it. In the language of theologians the term "superstition" tends to be confusing because it expresses two entirely different ideas, namely, a wrong application of religious sentiment, on the one hand, and a belief in unreal or ineffectual things, on the other; thus spiritualism is called "superstition", but rightly so only with respect to its interpretations of phenomena and its cult, and not with respect to the phenomena themselves; on the other hand sciences like astrology are perfectly real and effectual and imply no deviation of a pseudo-religious kind. The term "superstition" should really not be applied to sciences or facts that people ignore and ridicule without understanding them at all, but to practices which are either intrinsically useless or totally misunderstood and which are called upon to make up for the absence of spiritual attitudes or effectual rites; no less superstitious is a false or improper interpretation of a symbol or some coincidence, often in conjunction with fantastic fears or scruples, and so on. In these days the word "superstition" no longer means anything; when theologians use it—the point bears repetition—one never knows whether they are censuring a concrete diabolism or a mere illusion; for them a magical act and a pretence at magic look like the same thing, and they do not notice the contradiction inherent in declaring in the same breath that sorcery is a great sin and that it is nothing but superstition.

But let us return to the scientific naiveté of the men of old: according to Saint Thomas Aquinas, "an error concerning the creation engenders a false science of God"; this does not mean that knowledge of God demands a total knowledge of cosmic phenomena—a completely unrealizable condition in any case—but that our knowledge must be either symbolically true or physically adequate; in the second case it must retain for us a symbolic intelligibility, for without this all science is vain and harmful. For example, human science has the right to stop short at, or restrict itself to, the view that the earth is flat and that the heavens revolve, since the spiritual symbolism reflects adequately a real situation; but the evolutionary hypothesis is a proposition at once false and pernicious, since—besides being contrary to the nature of things—it deprives man of his essential significance and at the same stroke ruins the intelligibility of the world. In any human science dealing with phenomena, there is always an element of error; we cannot attain to more than a relative knowledge in this domain, but taken as a whole this can be sufficient in the context of our spiritual science. The ancients knew the laws of a nature that can be perceived directly: their astronomy was founded more or less on appearances, and though it included errors in the material field—but not in the spiritual field, since appearances are providential and have a meaning for us—this deficiency is largely compensated for by the comprehensiveness of traditional knowledge, which in fact takes account of Angels, Paradises, demons, hells, and the non-evolutionary spontaneity of the creation—that is, the crystallization of celestial Ideas in the cosmic substance—as well as the apocalyptic end of the world and many other such facts; these facts, whatever their mythical vesture, are essential to human beings. On the other hand, a science that denies them, prodigious though it may be in the material observation of sensible phenomena, could never claim the principle enunciated by Saint Thomas, first because a knowledge of essential things takes precedence over a knowledge of secondary things, and second because a knowledge that excludes the essentials of creation, both in fact and in principle, is incomparably more remote from an exact and complete adequation to truth than a science that is apparently "naive" but whole.

If it is "naive" to believe—because one sees it that way—that the earth is flat and that the sky and stars revolve around it, it is no less "naive" to take the world of the senses to be the only world, or the whole world, and to believe that matter—or energy if one prefers—is Existence as such; such errors are indeed incomparably greater than that of the geocentric system. Furthermore, the materialist and evolutionary error is, it must be insisted, immeasurably harmful, whereas a primitive and "natural" cosmology is nothing of the kind; this shows that there is no common measure at all between the insufficiency of the ancient cosmography and the overall—we do not say "partial"—falsity of a Promethean and titanic science, whose principle was bequeathed to us from the decadence of Greece.

And this is characteristic of the ravages of scientism and its special psychology: if one remarks to a convinced believer in progress that man could not possibly endure psychologically the conditions on another planet—and there is talk of colonizing other planets to relieve terrestrial over-population—he will answer without batting an eyelid that a new kind of man with the necessary qualities will be produced; such unawareness and insensibility are not far from the inhuman and monstrous, for to deny what is total and inalienable in man is to scoff at the divine intention that makes us what we are and that has consecrated our nature through the "Word made flesh". Tacitus laughed at the Germans who tried to stop a torrent with their shields, but it is no less naive to believe in planetary migration or to believe in the establishment by purely human means of a society fully satisfied and perfectly inoffensive, and continuing to progress indefinitely. All this proves that man, though he has inevitably become less naive in some things, has nevertheless learned nothing as far as essentials are concerned, to say the least; the only thing that man left to himself is capable of is to "commit the oldest sins the newest kind of ways", as Shakespeare would say. And the world being what it is, one is doubtless not guilty of a truism in adding that it is better to go to Heaven naively than to go intelligently to hell.

*   *   *

When one tries to reconstruct the psychology of the men of old, one nearly always makes the serious mistake of failing to take into account the inward repercussions of the corresponding outward manifestations: what matters is not a superficial improvement but the effectiveness of our attitudes toward the Invisible and the Absolute. Ways of thinking and acting that may sometimes surprise us by their appearance of ingenuousness—especially in the lives of the saints—often conceal an efficacy that is for that very reason all the more profound; despite the fact that in more recent times man has accumulated a mass of experience and much cleverness, he is certainly less "authentic" and less "effectual", or less sensitive to the influx of the supernatural, than were his distant ancestors; though he may smile—he the "civilized" man who has become "adult"—at some apparently artless piece of reasoning or at an attitude that is *a priori* childish or "pre-logical", the inward effectiveness of these points of reference eludes him. It never seems to occur to historians and psychologists that the surface components of human behavior are always relative and that a plus or a minus on that plane alone is never decisive, since only the internal mechanism of our contact with higher states or celestial prolongations is of real importance; the mental distance between a living "primitive" and a "civilized" person is regarded as equivalent to thousands of years, but experience proves that this distance, where it exists, is equivalent to no more than a few days, for man is everywhere and always man.

*   *   *

It is not naiveté and superstition alone that shift their position; intelligence does so as well, and they all move together; it is possible to satisfy oneself of this by reading philosophical texts or art criticism, where an obstinate individualism strides upon the stilts of a pretentious pseudo-psychology; it is as if one wished to borrow the subtlety of a Scholastic and the sensitivity of a troubadour in order to say whether the temperature is hot or cold. A monstrous expenditure of mental ability is incurred in setting out opinions that have no relation to intelligence; those who are not well endowed intellectually by nature learn how to play at thinking and cannot even manage without this imposture, whereas those who are well endowed are in danger of losing their ability to think by falling in with the trend. What looks like an ascent is really a descent: ignorance and lack of intelligence are at ease in a wholly superficial refinement, and the result is a climate in which wisdom takes on the appearance of naiveté, uncouthness, and reverie.

In our day everyone wants to appear intelligent; one would prefer to be accused of crime than of naiveté if the accompanying risks could be avoided. But since intelligence cannot be drawn from the void, subterfuges are resorted to, one of the most prevalent being the mania for "demystification", which allows an air of intelligence to be conveyed at small cost, for all one need do is assert that the normal response to a particular phenomenon is "prejudiced" and that it is high time it was cleared of the "legends" surrounding it; if the ocean could be made out to be a pond or the Himalayas a hill, it would be done. Certain writers find it impossible to be content with taking note of the fact that a particular thing or person has a particular character or destiny, as everyone had done before them; they must always begin by remarking that "it has too often been said", and go on to declare that the reality is something quite different and has at last been discovered, and that up till now all the world has been "living a lie". This strategy is applied above all to things that are evident and universally known; it would doubtless be too naive to acknowledge in so many words that a lion is a carnivore and that he is not quite safe to meet.

However that may be, there is naiveté everywhere and there always has been, and man cannot escape from it, unless he can surpass his humanity; in this truth lie the key and solution to the problem. For what matters is not the question of knowing whether the dialectic or demeanor of a Plato is naive or not, or whether they are so to a certain extent and no further—and one would like to know where the absolute standards of all this could be found—but exclusively the fact that the sage or the saint has an inward access to concrete Truth; the simplest formulation—doubtless the most "naive" for some tastes—can be the threshold of a Knowledge as complete and profound as possible.[1]

---

[1] "Blessed are the poor in spirit: for theirs is the kingdom of Heaven" (Matt. 5:3); "But let your communication be, Yea, yea; Nay, nay: for whatsoever is more than these cometh of evil" (Matt. 5:37); "Except ye be converted, and become as little children, ye shall not enter into the kingdom of Heaven" (Matt. 18:3); "Blessed are they that have not seen, and yet have believed" (John 20:29).

If the Bible is naive, it is an honor to be naive; if the philosophies that deny the Spirit are intelligent, there is no such thing as intelligence. Behind a humble belief in a Paradise situated among the clouds there is at least a foundation of inalienable truth, but more than that—and this is something priceless—there is a merciful reality that never disappoints.

Man in the Universe

Modern science, which is rationalist as to its subject and materialist as to its object, can describe our situation physically and approximately, but it can tell us nothing about our extra-spatial situation in the total and real Universe. Astronomers know more or less where we are in space, in what relative "place", in which of the peripheral arms of the Milky Way, and perhaps they may know where the Milky Way is situated among the other assemblages of star-dust; but they do not know where we are in existential "space", namely, in a state of hardening and at the center or summit of it, while at the same time being on the edge of an immense "rotation", which is none other than the current of forms, the "samsaric" flow of phenomena, the πάντα ῥεῖ* of Heraclitus. Profane science, in seeking to pierce to its depths the mystery of the things that contain—space, time, matter, energy—forgets the mystery of the things that are contained: it tries to explain the quintessential properties of our bodies and the intimate functioning of our souls, but it does not know what existence and intelligence are; consequently, given its principles, it cannot be otherwise than ignorant of what man is.

When we look around us, what do we see? First, existence; second, differences; third, movements, modifications, transformations; fourth, disappearances. All these things together manifest a state of universal Substance: this state is at once a crystallization and a rotation, a heaviness and a dispersion, a solidification and a segmentation. Just as water is in ice and the movement of the hub in the rim, so is God in phenomena; He is accessible in them and through them, this being the whole mystery of symbolism and of immanence. God is "the Outward" and "the Inward", "the First" and "the Last".[1]

God is the most dazzlingly evident of all evident things. Everything has a center; therefore the totality of things—the world—also has a center. We are at the periphery of "something absolute", and that "something" cannot be less powerful, less conscious, less intel-

---

* Translator's note: *panta rhei* ("all things flow") in English transliteration.
[1] Koranic divine Names: *az-Zâhir* and *al-Bâtin*, *al-Awwal* and *al-Âkhir*.

ligent than ourselves. Men think they have "solid earth" under their feet and that they possess a real power; they feel perfectly "at home" on earth and attach much importance to themselves, whereas they know neither whence they came nor whither they are going and are drawn through life as by an invisible cord.

All things are limited. Now to say limitation is to say effect, and to say effect is to say cause; thus it is that all things, by their limitation no less than by their content, prove God, the first and therefore limitless Cause.

Or again: what proves the Absolute extrinsically? In the first place the relative, since it is meaningless without the absoluteness it restricts, and in the second place the "relatively absolute", that is, the reflection of the Absolute in the relative. The question of intrinsic or direct proofs of the Absolute does not arise, the evidence being in the Intellect itself and thus in all our being, so that indirect proofs can do no more than serve as supports or occasional causes; in the Intellect, subject and object mingle or interpenetrate in a certain fashion. Certitude exists in fact, or else the word would not exist; there is therefore no reason to deny it on the plane of pure intellection and of the universal.[2]

*   *   *

The ego is at the same time a system of images and a cycle; it is something like a museum, and a unique and irreversible journey through that museum. The ego is a moving fabric made of images and tendencies; the tendencies come from our own substance, and the images are furnished by the environment. We put ourselves into things, and we place things in ourselves, whereas our true being is independent of them.

Alongside this system of images and tendencies that constitutes our ego there is a myriad of other systems of images and tendencies. Some of them are worse or less beautiful than our own, and others are better or more beautiful.

We are like foam ceaselessly renewed on the ocean of Existence. But since God has put Himself into this foam, it is destined to become a sea of stars at the time of the final crystallization of spirits.

---

[2] Modern philosophy is a liquidation of evidences, and therefore fundamentally of intelligence; it is no longer in any degree a *sophia*, but rather a "misosophy".

The tiny system of images must become, when its terrestrial contingency is left behind, a star immortalized in the halo of Divinity. This star can be conceived on various levels; the divine Names are its archetypes; beyond the stars burns the Sun of the Self in its blazing transcendence and in infinite peace.

Man does not choose; he follows his nature and his vocation, and it is God who chooses.

*   *   *

A man who has fallen into the mire, and who knows that he can get out in this way or that and with a certain effort, does not think of rebelling against natural laws nor of cursing existence; it is obvious to him that mud can exist and that there is such a thing as weight, and he only thinks of getting out of the mire. Now, we are in the mire of earthly existence, and we know we can escape from it, whatever trials we may undergo: Revelation gives us this assurance, and the Intellect is able to take this into account *a posteriori*. It is therefore absurd to deny God and to abuse the world for the sole reason that existence presents fissures, which it cannot but present, on pain of not existing and not being able to "existentiate".

We are situated as it were under a sheet of ice that neither our five senses nor our reason enable us to pierce, but the Intellect—at once a mirror of the supra-sensible and itself a supernatural ray of light—passes through this ice without difficulty once Revelation has allowed it to become conscious of its own nature; religious belief also passes through this cosmic shell, in a less direct and more affective manner no doubt, but nonetheless intuitively in many cases; the divine Mercy, which is contained in universal Reality and which proves the fundamentally "beneficent"[3] character of that Reality, desires moreover that Revelation should intervene wherever that sheet of ice or that shell exists, so much so that we are never completely shut in, except in our refusal of Mercy. Mistaking the ice that imprisons us for Reality, we do not acknowledge what it excludes and experience no desire for deliverance; we try to compel the ice to be happiness. Within the order of physical laws nobody thinks of refusing the Mercy that dwells indirectly in the nature of things: no man on the point of drowning refuses the pole held out to him; but

[3] Although the divine nature is beyond moral specifications.

too many men refuse Mercy in the total order because it surpasses the narrow bounds of their daily experience and the no less narrow limits of their understanding. Man does not in general want to be saved except on condition that he need not surpass himself.

The fact that we are imprisoned in our five senses contains within itself an aspect of Mercy, paradoxical though this may seem after what has just been said. If the number of our senses were multiplied—and theoretically there is no limit in principle to their multiplication—objective reality would tear through us like a hurricane; it would break us in pieces and crush us at the same time. Our "vital space" would be transparent; we would be as if suspended over an abyss or as if rushed through an incommensurable macrocosm, with its entrails exposed so to speak, and filled with terror; instead of living in a maternal, charitably opaque, and watertight compartment of the universe—for the world is a womb and death a cruel birth—we would find ourselves forever faced with a totality of spaces or abysses and a myriad of creatures and phenomena, such that no individual could possibly endure the experience. Man is made for the Absolute or the Infinite, not for limitless contingency.

Man, we have said, is as if buried under a sheet of ice. His experience of it takes various forms: at one time it is the cosmic ice that matter has become in its present and post-Edenic state of solidity, and at another time it is the ice of ignorance.

Goodness is in the very substance of the Universe, and for that reason it penetrates right into the matter we know, "accursed" though that matter may be; the fruits of the earth and the rain from the sky, which make life possible, are nothing if not manifestations of the Goodness which penetrates everywhere and warms the world, and which we carry within ourselves, in the depths of our chilled hearts.

*　　*　　*

The symbolism of a fountain reminds us that all things are by definition an exteriorization projected into a void in itself non-existent, but nevertheless perceptible in phenomena; water, in this imagery, is the "stuff that dreams are made on" (Shakespeare), which produces worlds and beings. The distance of the water drops from their source corresponds on the macrocosmic scale to a principle of coagulation and hardening, and also on a certain plane to a principle of individuation; the weight that makes the drops fall back is then the supernatural attraction of the divine Center. The image of the fountain does not however take into account the degrees of reality nor especially the absolute transcendence of the Center or the Principle; what is does take into account is the unity of "substance" or of "non-unreality",[4] but not the existential separation that cuts the relative off from the Absolute; the first relationship goes from the Principle to manifestation and the second from manifestation to the Principle; in other words there is unity "from the point of view" of the Principle and diversity or separativity from the point of view of creatures inasmuch as they are only themselves.

In a certain sense worlds are like living bodies, and beings are like the blood or air that courses through them; the contents as well as the containers are "illusory" projections out of the Principle— illusory since in reality nothing can be separated from it—but the contents are dynamic and the containers static; this distinction is not apparent in the symbolism of the fountain, but it is apparent in the symbolism of respiration or the circulation of the blood.

The sage looks at things in connection with their necessarily imperfect and ephemeral exteriorization, but he also looks at them in connection with their perfect and eternal content. In a moral and therefore strictly human and volitive context, this exteriorization coincides indirectly with the idea of "sin",[5] and this is something that man, insofar as he is an active and passional creature, must never lose sight of.

*   *   *

There has been much speculation on the question of knowing how the sage—the "gnostic"[6] or *jnânin*—"sees" the world of phenomena, and occultists of all sorts have not refrained from putting forward the most fantastic theories on "clairvoyance" and the "third eye"; but

---

[4] That is to say, nothing can be situated outside the only Reality.

[5] "All that becomes deserves to perish," says Goethe in *Faust*; but he is mistaken in attributing the destructive function to the devil, whose role is in reality restricted to perversion and subversion.

[6] This word, here and elsewhere, is used in its etymological sense and has nothing to do with anything that may historically be called "Gnosticism". It is *gnosis* itself that is in question and not its pseudo-religious deviations.

in reality the difference between ordinary vision and that enjoyed by the sage or gnostic is obviously not of the sensorial order. The sage sees things in their total context, therefore in their relativity and at the same time in their metaphysical transparency; he does not see them as if they were physically diaphanous or endowed with a mystical sonority or a visible aura, even though his vision may sometimes be described by means of such images. If we see before us a landscape and we know it to be a mirage—even if the eye alone cannot discern its true nature—we look at it otherwise than we would if it were a real landscape; a star makes a different impression on us from a firefly, even when the optical circumstances are such that the sensation is the same for the eye; the sun would fill us with terror if it ceased to set.[7] It is thus that a spiritual vision of things is distinguished by a concrete perception of universal relationships and not by some special sensorial characteristic. The "third eye" is the faculty of seeing phenomena *sub specie aeternitatis* and therefore in a sort of simultaneity; to it are often added, in the nature of things, intuitions concerning modalities that are in practice imperceptible.

The sage sees causes in effects and effects in causes; he sees God in all things and all things in God. A science that penetrates the depths of the "infinitely great" and the "infinitely small" on the physical plane and yet denies other planes, even though it is they that reveal the sufficient reason of the nature we perceive and provide its key, is a greater evil than ignorance pure and simple; it is in fact a "counter-science", and its ultimate effects cannot but be deadly. In other words modern science is a totalitarian rationalism, which eliminates both Revelation and Intellect, and at the same time a totalitarian materialism, which ignores the metaphysical relativity—and hence the impermanence—of matter and the world; it does not know that the supra-sensible—which is beyond space and time—is the concrete principle of the world, and that it is consequently also at the origin of that contingent and changeable coagulation called "matter".[8] The science called "exact"[9] is in fact

---

[7] It is not for nothing that the Vedantists describe ignorance as "mistaking a rope for a serpent".

[8] Recent interpretations may perhaps "refine" the idea of matter, but they do not rise above its level in the smallest degree.

[9] It is not really "exact" since it denies everything that it cannot prove on its own ground and by its own methods, as if the impossibility of material or mathematical proofs were a proof of non-existence.

an "intelligence without wisdom", just as post-scholastic philosophy is conversely a "wisdom without intelligence".

The principle of individuation produces a succession of spiritual outlooks that become ever narrower. First of all, beyond this principle, there is the intrinsic vision of Divinity: it consists in seeing only God. The next stage in descending order is to see all things in Him, and next again to see God in all things; in a certain sense these two ways of seeing are equivalent or nearly so. After this comes the wholly indirect "vision" of the ordinary man: things "and" God; and finally there is the ignorance that sees only things and excludes God, which amounts to saying that it reduces the Principle to manifestation or the Cause to the effect. But in reality God alone sees Himself; to see God is to see by Him.

One must know what contains and not become dispersed among the contents. What contains is above all the permanent miracle of existence, then the miracle of consciousness or intelligence, and then the miracle of joy, which—like an expansive and creative power—fills as it were the existential and intellectual "spaces". All that is not capable of immortality will be burned: accidents perish; Reality alone remains.

There is in every man an incorruptible star—a substance called upon to become crystallized in Immortality and eternally prefigured in the luminous proximity of the Self. This star man can set free only in truth, in prayer, and in virtue.

The Universality and Timeliness of Monasticism

Finding a common denominator for phenomena as varied as the different monasticisms of the West and the East does not appear at first an easy task, for in order to be able to define, one must have found a point of view that makes definition possible; now it seems to us that this point of view arises simply from the nature of things, seeing that it is impossible to provide an account of human nature without relating it back to its divine conditions, or of the human phenomenon without connecting it either positively or negatively to God; for without God man is nothing. We can therefore say that the effort to reduce the complexity of life to a simple, but essential and liberating, formula comes from whatever is most complete and profound in the human condition and that this effort has led—in the most diverse spiritual climates—to the sort of institutional sanctity that constitutes monasticism.

Man was created alone, and he dies alone; monasticism aspires to preserve this solitude in its metaphysically irreplaceable aspect; it aims to restore to man his primordial solitude before God, or again it wishes to bring man back to his spiritual integrity and totality. A perfect society would be a society of hermits, if such a paradox may be permitted; now this is exactly what the monastic community seeks to realize, for monasticism is in a certain sense an organized eremitism.

The reflections that follow may seem to be truisms to some people, but they concern mental habits so ineradicable that it is difficult to underestimate their importance if one looks at things in depth. The point at issue is this: according to current opinion, monasticism is a matter of "vocation", but not in the proper sense of the word; when a man is simple enough to take religion literally and commits the indiscretion of allowing rather too spiritual opinions or attitudes to appear, people do not scruple to tell him that he belongs "in a monastery", as if he were a foreign body with no right to existence outside the walls of an appropriate institution. The idea of "vocation", which in itself is positive, then becomes negative: a man is said to be "called" not insofar as he is in the truth and because he is so, but because he disturbs society by causing it to become involuntarily aware of what it is. According to this more

or less conventional way of looking at things, an absence of vocation—or let us say worldliness—exists *de jure* and not merely *de facto*,
which means that perfection then seems like an optional specialty,
hence a luxury; it is reserved for monks, but one forgets to ask why
it is not for everyone.

A monk will certainly never blame anyone simply for living in
the world; this is self-evident, given the existence of secular clergy
and lay saints; what is blameworthy is not living "in the world",
but living in it badly and thus in a certain sense creating it. When
anyone reproaches a hermit or a monk for "fleeing" the world, he
commits a double error: first, he loses sight of the fact that contemplative isolation has an intrinsic value independent of the existence
of a surrounding "world"; second, he pretends to forget that there
are forms of flight which are perfectly honorable: if it is neither
absurd nor shameful to do one's best to escape an avalanche, it is
no more so to run away from the temptations or even simply the
distractions of the world, or from our own ego to the extent it is
rooted in this vicious circle; and let us not forget that in disencum-
bering ourselves of the world we disencumber the world of our own
sufferings. In our day people are very ready to say that to flee the
world is to shirk "responsibilities", a completely hypocritical euphemism that conceals spiritual laziness and a hatred of the absolute
behind "altruistic" or "social" ideas; people are happy to ignore the
fact that the gift of oneself to God is always the gift of oneself to all.
It is metaphysically impossible to give oneself to God without this
resulting in something good for the environment; to give oneself to
God—though it were hidden from all—is to give oneself to man, for
this gift of self has a sacrificial value of an incalculable radiance.

From another point of view, to work for one's own salvation
is like breathing, eating, sleeping; one cannot do these things for
anyone else nor help anyone else by abstaining from them. Egoism
is taking away from others what they need; it is not taking for oneself something of which they know nothing or for which they have
no desire.

Monasticism is not situated outside the world; it is the world that
situates itself outside monasticism: if every man lived in the love of
God, the monastery would be everywhere, and it is in this sense one
can say that every saint is implicitly a monk or hermit. Or again:
just as it is possible to introduce the "world" into the framework of
monasticism, since not every monk is a saint, so also it is possible to

transfer monasticism—or the attitude it represents—into the world, for there can be contemplatives anywhere.

*   *   *

If we define monasticism as a "withdrawal for God" while acknowledging its universal and inter-religious character—for a thirst for the supernatural is in the nature of normal man—how can we apply this definition to spiritual Muslims, who do not withdraw from society, or to Buddhists, who do cut themselves off but do not seem to have the idea of God? In other words—as far as Islam is concerned—how can there be a spirituality in a religion that rejects monasticism, or again why is monasticism excluded from a religion that nevertheless possesses mysticism, ascetic disciplines, and a cult of saints? To this we must reply that one of the reasons for Islam is precisely the possibility of a "monastery-society", if one may express it so: that is, Islam aims to carry the contemplative life into the very framework of society as a whole; within that framework, it succeeds in realizing conditions of structure and behavior that allow for contemplative isolation in the very midst of the activities of the world. It must be added that what corresponds to the monastery for the Muslim is above all an initiatic attachment to a brotherhood and submission—*perinde ac cadaver*—to a spiritual master, as well as the practice of supererogatory orisons together with vigils and fasts; the isolating element with respect to the worldly is strictness in observation of the *sunnah*; this strictness—which the surrounding society would not think of opposing in a Muslim country—is equivalent in practice to the walls of a monastery. It is true that dervishes assemble in their *zâwiyah*s for their communal practices and make retreats in them lasting sometimes for several months; a few live there and consecrate their whole lives to prayer and service of the *shaykh*; but the result is not monasticism in a strict sense, comparable to that of Christians or Buddhists. Be that as it may, the famous "no monasticism in Islam" (*lâ rahbâniyah fi'l-islâm*) does not really mean that contemplatives must not withdraw from the world, but on the contrary that the world must not be withdrawn from contemplatives; the intrinsic ideal of monasticism or eremitism—namely, asceticism and the mystical life—is in no way in question. And let us not forget that "holy war" is accompanied in Islam by the same mystical development as in Christian chivalry, notably that of the

103

Templars; it offers a way of sacrifice and martyrdom, which united Christians and Muslims at the time of the crusades in one and the same sacrificial love of God.

In the case of Buddhism the difficulty lies in the fact that this religion, while it is essentially monastic—and is so to a degree that cannot be surpassed—seems to ignore the idea of God; now it goes without saying that an "atheistic spirituality" is a contradiction in terms, and in fact Buddhism possesses completely the idea of a transcendent Absolute, just as it possesses the idea of a contact between this Absolute and man. If Buddhism does not have the idea of a "God" in the Semitic or Aryan sense of the word, it is nonetheless just as conscious in its own way of divine Reality, for it is far from ignoring the crucial ideas of absoluteness, transcendence, perfection, and—on the human side—of sacrifice and sanctity; though doubtless "non-theist", it is certainly not "atheist". The aspect of a "personal God" appears notably in the Mahayanic cult of the Buddha Amitabha—Japanese Amidism—where it is combined with a perspective of redemptive Mercy; Christian influences have been suggested, which is not only false, but even implausible from more than one point of view; it is forgotten that it is in accordance with the fundamental nature of things that phenomena analogous at least in their forms should occur wherever circumstances are favorable. This prejudice concerning "influences" or "borrowings" makes us think of the ethnographer who found among the Red Indians the myth of the flood and ingenuously concluded that missionaries had been in touch with them, whereas this myth—or rather this recollection—is found among almost all the peoples of the earth.

These last remarks give us the opportunity of saying a few words about the current confusion between syncretism and eclecticism, although this may carry us a little away from our subject. Syncretism is never something substantial: it is an assembling of heterogeneous elements into a false unity, that is, a unity without real synthesis; eclecticism on the other hand is natural wherever different doctrines exist side by side, as is proven by the integration of Platonism or Aristotelianism into the Christian perspective. What is important in such a case is that the original perspective remain faithful to itself and accept foreign concepts only to the extent they corroborate its faithfulness by helping to elucidate the fundamental intentions of its own perspective; Christians had no reason not to be inspired by Greek wisdom since it was at hand, just as Muslims could not prevent themselves from using Neoplatonic concepts in their mystical doctrine—at least to a certain extent—as soon as they became aware of them; but it would be a serious error to speak of syncretism in these cases by mistakenly recalling the example of such artificial doctrines as those of modern theosophy. There have never been borrowings between two living religions of essential elements affecting their fundamental structures, as is imagined when Amidism is attributed to the Nestorians.

The monasticism of Hindus and Taoists should also be mentioned as Asian examples, but they can scarcely be said to present difficulties comparable to those we have considered in connection with Islam and Buddhism; of course there is always the difficulty of religious differences in general, but this is a complex problem which our present somewhat synthetic survey of monasticism as a phenomenon of humanity need not take into account.

*   *   *

A world is absurd to the extent that the contemplative, the hermit, the monk appear in it as a paradox or "anachronism". Now the monk is timely precisely because he is timeless: we live in an epoch characterized by an idolatry of "the times", and the monk incarnates all that is changeless, not through sclerosis or inertia, but through transcendence.

And this leads us to introduce certain issues that bring negatively into relief the burning timeliness of the monastic ideal—or simply the religious ideal, which in the final analysis amounts to the same thing. In the world of absurd relativism that we live in, anyone who says "our times" thinks he has said everything; to identify phenomena of any kind with "other times" or still more with "times gone by" is to liquidate them; and consider the hypocritical sadism concealed by such words as "bygone", "outdated", or "irreversible", which replace thought by a sort of imaginative suggestion—a "music of prejudice", we might say. People take note, for example, that some liturgical or ceremonial practice offends the scientistic or demagogic tastes of our age, and they are relieved when they recall that the usage in question dates from the Middle Ages, or perhaps that it is "Byzantine", because this allows them to conclude without further ado that it no longer has any right to existence; they completely forget that there is only one question to be asked, namely, *why* the Byzantines did such a thing; more often than not one finds that this "why" is located outside of time and that its reason for being is connected to timeless factors. Identifying oneself with an "age" and removing from things all, or nearly all, their intrinsic worth is quite a new attitude, one which is arbitrarily projected into what we retrospectively call "the past"; in reality our ancestors did not live in a time, speaking subjectively and intellectually, but in a "space", that is, in a world of stable values in which the flux of duration was only accidental so to speak; they had a marvelous sense of the absolute in things and of the rootedness of things in the absolute.

Our age tends more and more to cut man off from his roots; but in seeking to "start again from scratch" and to reduce man to the purely human it succeeds only in dehumanizing him, which proves that the "purely human" is only a fiction; man is fully man only in rising above himself, and he can do so only through religion. Monasticism is there to remind us that man is human only by virtue of his permanent consciousness of the Absolute and absolute values and that the works of man are nothing in themselves; the desert Fathers, Cassian, Saint Benedict, and others have shown that before acting one must be and that actions are precious to the extent that the love of God animates them or is reflected in them and tolerable to the extent that they are not opposed to this love. The fullness of being, which depends on the spirit, can in principle dispense with action; action does not carry its end in itself: Martha is certainly not superior to Mary. Man is distinguished from the animals in two essential respects, first by his intelligence, which has a capacity for the absolute and thus for objectivity and a sense of the relative, and then by his free will, which is capable of choosing God and attaching itself to Him; the rest is only contingency, especially this profane and quantitative "culture", of which the early Church had no conception and which is now made into a mainstay of human value, in defiance of current experience and contrary to fact.

In our age man is defined not by reference to his specific nature—which is definable only in a divine context—but by reference to the inextricable consequences of an already secular Prometheanism: it is human works, or even the remote consequences of these works, which in the minds of our contemporaries determine and define man. We live in a scene-shifter's world in which it has become almost impossible to make contact with the primordial realities of things; prejudices and reflexes dictated by an irreversible slide intervene at every step; it is as if before the Renaissance or the Encyclopedists man had not been wholly man, or as if in order to be man it were necessary to have passed by way of Descartes, Voltaire, Rousseau, Kant, Marx, Darwin, and Freud, not forgetting—most recent of all—the lethal Teilhard de Chardin. It is sad to see how religious convictions are all too often enveloped in an irreligious sensibility or how such convictions are accompanied by reflexes directly opposed to them; apologetics tends more and more to take its stand on the wrong ground, on which its victory is in any case impossible, and to adopt a language that rings false and is able to convince no one, with the exception of an occasional propagandist success that in no way serves religion as such; when apologetics brushes up against demagogy it enters upon the road to suicide. Instead of keeping to the pure and simple truth—a truth that quite obviously cannot please everyone—people allow themselves to be fascinated by the postulates of the adversary as well as his self-assurance, dynamism, easy success, and efficient vulgarity; on the pretext of not wanting to "confiscate" the religious message, it is extrinsically and imperceptibly "falsified", though one carefully avoids believing in this danger and mentioning this word; the very most that is admitted is the danger of "attenuating the message", a euphemism in which the bias is evident.

"Have dominion over the earth," says the Bible, and progressivists miss no chance of exploiting this sentence to justify the ever more totalitarian industrialism of our age and to extol a corresponding "spirituality"; in reality it is a very long time since man has obeyed this injunction of the Creator; in order to grasp its true intention and limits, it is necessary to remember the divine command to "take no thought for the morrow" and similar injunctions.[1] It is pure hypocrisy to make much of the Biblical sentence first quoted without situating it in its total context, for according to this logic it would also be right to attribute an absolute force to the words "be fruitful and multiply"[2] and abolish all chastity in Christianity or even to return to the polygamy of the Hebrews. This strange eagerness

---

[1] "For what is a man profited, if he shall gain the whole world, and lose his own soul?" (Matt. 16:26).

[2] "Be fruitful, and multiply, and replenish the earth, and subdue it; and have dominion over the fish of the sea, and over the fowl of the air, and over every living thing that moveth upon the earth" (Gen. 1:28).

to follow the "commandments of God" might well lead—it seems
to us—to many other scriptural discoveries besides that of a passage concerning agriculture, fishing, hunting, and stock-rearing
and to many spiritual concerns other than the industrialization of
religion.[3]

*   *   *

Inferiority complexes and mimetic reflexes are bad counselors: how
often one meets with absurd reproaches leveled not only at the
religion of the Middle Ages but also at that of the nineteenth century, which even then was still not "atomic", as if all men who lived
before ourselves had been struck with an inexplicable blindness
and as if it had been necessary to await the advent of a given atheistic philosopher to discover a light both decisive and mysteriously
unknown to all the saints. It is too readily forgotten that, if human
nature has a right to its shortcomings today, which no one disputes,
it had the same right to them in the past; "progress" is most often a
mere transference, the exchange of one evil for another; otherwise
our age would be perfect and sanctified. In the human world as
such, it is scarcely possible to choose a good; one is always reduced
to choosing a lesser evil, and to determine which evil is the lesser
we are obliged to refer to a hierarchy of values derived from eternal
realities, and this is exactly what "our age" never does. In the Middle
Ages one started from the idea that man is bad because he is a
sinner, whereas in our century man is good since sin does not exist,
the reversal being so complete that evil is above all whatever makes
us believe in sin; modern humanitarianism, convinced that man is
good, purports to protect man, but from whom? Obviously from
man, but what man? And if evil does not come from man, from
whom does it come, given the conviction that nothing intelligent
exists outside the human being nor especially above him?

[3] The partisans of this "forcing into step" must be answered by the Scriptures:
"Whoso therefore will be a friend of the world is the enemy of God" (James 4:4).
"And be not conformed to this world: but be ye transformed by the renewing of
your mind, that ye may prove what is that good, and acceptable, and perfect, will
of God" (Rom. 12:2). In our day it is the other way round: it is atheistic scientism,
demagogy, the machine that decides what is good, what should be pleasing to God,
what is perfect. "Woe unto you, when all men shall speak well of you! for so did their
fathers to the false prophets" (Luke 6:26).

There is a prejudice of science and a prejudice of society; monasticism, with its insistence on the "one thing needful" and its collective pauperism, free from all envy—and perfectly concrete as far as individuals are concerned, though a monastery itself may be rich—offers in its own way the answer to these two obstacles. What is a science that takes account neither of the transcendent and conscious Infinite, nor the hereafter, nor such basic phenomena as Revelation, miracle, pure intellection, contemplation, sanctity; and what is a social equilibrium that abolishes all real superiority and takes no account of the intrinsic nature of man nor his ultimate destiny? People smile at the Biblical account of creation, but they pay no attention to Semitic symbolism, which furnishes the key to things apparently naive; it is claimed that the Church has always been "on the side of the rich", and it is forgotten that from the point of view of religion there is only man, whether rich or poor—man, made of flesh and spirit, always exposed to suffering and doomed to die; and if the Church as an earthly institution has been forced to lean on the powerful who protected her, or were supposed to protect her, she has never refused herself to the poor and utterly compensates for her accidental and human imperfections by her spiritual gifts and numberless saints, not forgetting that permanent spiritual presence which is precisely what monasticism actualizes. The Catholic Church has been reproached for its "self-sufficiency": now the Church has every reason for being "self-sufficient" since she is what she is and offers what she offers; it is not for her to fret, nor undertake her own "self-criticism", nor "catch up", as those who have no sense of her dignity wish. The Church has the right to repose in herself; her frontline troops are the saints; she has no need of busy demagogues who act out "drama" and "death-throes". The saints suffice her, and she has always had them.[4]

The success of atheistic materialism can be explained in part by the fact that it is an extreme position, an easy extremism given the tottering world that serves as its framework and the psychological elements to which it appeals. Christianity is also an extreme position, but instead of this fact being stressed it is concealed—this at least is the tendency that seems to prevail—and one adapts oneself

---

[4] And let us add in this regard that a Church which is not "triumphalist" is not a Church, any more than a dogma which is not "thunderous" is a dogma.

to the position of the adversary, whereas it is precisely the extremism of the Christian message, if it is affirmed without disguise—but also without any affected "dynamism"—which has the gift of fascinating and convincing. A conscious or unconscious capitulation before the arguments of the adversary evidently originates in a desire to give him the impression that the Christian absolute realizes the same sort of perfection as the progressivist and socialist absolute, and those aspects—however essential—of the Christian absolute are disowned which collide with opposing tendencies, with the result that nothing is left with which to counter those tendencies except a half-absolute devoid of all originality; for there are two false attitudes: saying that one has never had anything in view except social progress, which is a ridiculous falsehood wholly unrelated to the Christian perspective, or accusing oneself—while vowing to do better in the future—of having neglected social progress, which is a betrayal pure and simple; what ought to be done is to put each thing in its place and insist at every turn on what man, life, the world, and society are from the religious point of view. Christianity is an eschatological perspective, considering things in relation to the hereafter or not considering them at all; to pretend to adopt some other way of looking at things—or to adopt it in fact—while remaining within religion is incomprehensible and disastrous nonsense. The timeliness of monasticism is that it incarnates—whether one likes it or not—precisely the sort of thing which is extreme and absolute in religion and which is of a spiritual and contemplative essence; earthly charity has no meaning save in connection with heavenly charity. "Seek ye first the kingdom of God, and his righteousness."

It is evident and inevitable that religion can and sometimes must adapt itself to new circumstances; but care must be taken not to decide *a priori* in favor of circumstances and not to look upon them as norms simply because they exist and please a majority. In proceeding to an adaptation it is important to adhere strictly to the religious perspective and the hierarchy of values it implies; inspiration must come from a metaphysical and spiritual criteriology, and one must not give way to pressures or allow oneself to be contaminated by a false evaluation of things. Do we not hear of a "religion orientated toward the social", which is either a pleonasm or else an absurdity, and even of a "spirituality of economic development", which—apart from its monstrosity—is a contradiction in terms? According to this way of thinking, error or sin need no longer be subordinated to the imperatives of truth and spirituality; on the contrary it is truth and spirituality that must be adapted to error and sin; and it is the opinion of the adversary that is the criterion of truth and falsehood, of good and evil.

*   *   *

But let us return for a moment to the modern scientific outlook since it plays so decisive a role in the contemporary mentality; we see absolutely no reason for going into raptures about space flights; the saints in their ecstasies climb infinitely higher, and we do not say this in an allegorical vein, but in a perfectly concrete sense that could be called "scientific" or "exact". In vain does modern science explore the infinitely distant and the infinitely small; in its own way it can reach the world of galaxies and that of molecules, but since it believes neither in Revelation nor pure intellection, it is unaware of all the immaterial and supra-sensory worlds which envelop as it were our sensory dimension and in relation to which these dimensions are no more than a sort of fragile coagulation, destined to vanish at its appointed time before the dazzling power of divine Reality. Now to postulate a science without a metaphysics is a flagrant contradiction, for without metaphysics there can be neither standards nor criteria, no intelligence that penetrates, contemplates, and coordinates. Both relativistic psychologism, which ignores the absolute, and evolutionism—which is absurd because contradictory, since the greater cannot come from the less—can be explained only by this exclusion of what is essential and total in intelligence.

In times past it was the object that was sometimes doubted, including the object that can be found in ourselves—an "object" being anything of which the subject can be distinctively and separatively conscious, even a moral defect in the subject—but in our day no one fears the contradiction of doubting the knowing subject in its intrinsic and irreplaceable aspect; intelligence as such is called into question, even "examined", without anyone wondering "who" examines it—is there not talk about producing a more perfect man?—and without taking account of the fact that philosophic doubt is included in this same devaluation, that it falls with the fall of intelligence, and that at the same stroke all science and philosophy collapse. For if our intelligence is by definition ineffectual, if we are irresponsible or lumps of earth, philosophy is useless.

What we are being pressed to admit is that our spirit is relative in its very essence, that this essence contains no stable standard of measurement—as if the sufficient reason of the human intellect were not precisely that it should comprise such standards!—and that the ideas of the true and the false are therefore intrinsically relative, hence always vacillating; and since certain consequences of accumulated errors collide with our innate standards and are unmasked and condemned by them, we are told that it is a question of habit and that we must change our nature—that we must create a new intelligence that finds beautiful what is ugly and accepts as true what is false. The devil is essentially incapable of recognizing that he is wrong unless such an admission is in his interest; it is thus error become habitual that must be right at all costs, even at the cost of our intelligence and in the final analysis of our existence; as for the nature of things and our faculty of adequation, this is all "prejudice".

It has been said and said again that monasticism in all its forms, whether Christian or Buddhist, is a manifestation of "pessimism"; thus through either convenience or carelessness, the intellectual and realistic aspect of the question is evaded and objective observations, metaphysical ideas, and logical conclusions are reduced to purely sentimental attitudes. A man who knows that an avalanche is an avalanche is accused of "pessimism", and one who thinks it is a mist is an "optimist"; to think serenely of death while scorning distractions is to see the world in dark colors, but to think of death with repugnance, or to avoid thinking of it at all, while finding all the happiness of which one is capable in passing things is "courage", it seems, and shows a "sense of responsibility". We have never understood why those who put their hope in God, while having enough discernment to be able to read the "signs of the times", are accused of bitterness whereas others are credited with strong and cheerful natures because they mistake mirages for realities; and it is almost incredible that this false optimism, which is completely opposed to the Scriptures on the one hand and to the most tangible of criteria on the other, should win over men who profess to believe in God and the future life.

*   *   *

We now wish to describe in a certain way—though there would be a thousand other ways of doing so—how a man who has attached himself to God is spiritually situated in existence or how he takes his stand when faced with the dizzying abyss that is the world. The condition of the monk—for it is he who most interests us here, though the same considerations could be applied to contemplatives in general—constitutes a victory over space and time, or over the world and life, in the sense that he places himself by his attitude at the center and in the present: at the center in relation to a world full of phenomena and in the present in relation to a life full of events. Concentration of prayer and rhythm of prayer: these are in a certain sense the two dimensions of spiritual existence in general and monastic existence in particular. The monk withdraws from the world, fixing himself in a definite place—a place that is center because it is consecrated to God—and morally he shuts his eyes and remains where he is, awaiting death like a statue set in a niche, as Saint Francis of Sales says; by this "concentration" the monk places himself beneath the divine axis, already partaking of Heaven by attaching himself concretely to God. In so doing the contemplative also withdraws from duration, for through prayer—that permanent actualization of consciousness of the Absolute—he is situated in a timeless instant: prayer—or the remembrance of God—is now and always, being "always now" and already belonging to Eternity. The life of the monk, by the elimination of disordered movements, is a rhythm; now rhythm is the fixation of an instant—or the present—in duration just as immobility is the fixation of a point—or the center—in space; this symbolism, founded as it is on the law of analogy, becomes concrete by virtue of a consecration to God. Thus it is that the monk holds the world in his hands and dominates life as well: for there is nothing precious in the world which we do not possess even here, provided that this point where we are belongs to God and that, being here for God, we belong to Him; and in the same way, all our life is in that instant in which we choose God and not vanities.

In the temporal dimension that stretches ahead of us there are only three certainties: death, Judgment, and eternal Life. We have no power over the past, and we do not know the future; as far as the future is concerned we have only these three certainties, but we possess a fourth in this very moment, and it is everything: it is that of our actuality, our present freedom to choose God and thus to choose our whole destiny. In this instant, this present, we hold our whole life, our whole existence: all is good if this instant is good and if we know how to place our life within this blessed instant; the whole secret of spiritual faithfulness lies in dwelling in this instant, in renewing and perpetuating it by prayer, in holding on to it by means of spiritual rhythm, in enclosing completely within it the time that floods over us and threatens to drag us far away from this "divine moment". The vocation of the monk is perpetual prayer, not because life is long, but because it is only a moment; the perpetuity—or the rhythm—of the orison demonstrates that life is merely an ever-present instant, just as spatial fixation in a consecrated place demonstrates that the world is merely a point, a point however which belongs to God and is therefore everywhere and excludes no felicity.

This condensation of the existential dimensions—insofar as they are indefinite and arbitrary—into a blessed unity is at the same time what constitutes the essence of man; the rest is contingency and accident. This is a truth that concerns every human being; thus the monk is not a being apart, but simply a prototype or model, or a spiritual diagram, a point of reference: every man—because he is a man—should realize in one way or another this victory over a world that disperses and a life that enslaves. Too many people think that they do not have time to pray, but this is an illusion that results from indifference, which—according to Fénelon—is the worst ailment of the soul; for the numerous moments we fill with our habitual dreams, including our all too often useless reflections, we take away from God and ourselves.

The great mission of monasticism is to show the world that happiness does not lie somewhere far away or in something located outside ourselves, in a treasure to be sought or in a world to be built, but precisely here where we belong to God. Faced with a dehumanized world, the monk represents what our true standards are; his mission is to remind men what man is.

Keys to the Bible

In order to understand the nature of the Bible and its meaning, it is essential to have recourse to the ideas of both symbolism and revelation; without an exact and, in the measure necessary, sufficiently profound understanding of these key ideas, the approach to the Bible remains hazardous and risks engendering grave doctrinal, psychological, and historical errors. Here it is above all the idea of revelation that is indispensable, for the literal meaning of the Bible, particularly in the Psalms and in the words of Jesus, affords sufficient food for piety apart from any question of symbolism; but this nourishment would lose all its vitality and all its liberating power without an adequate idea of revelation or of supra-human origin.

Other passages, particularly in Genesis, though also in texts such as the Song of Songs, remain an enigma in the absence of traditional commentaries. When approaching Scripture, one should always pay the greatest attention to rabbinical and cabalistic commentaries and—in Christianity—to the patristic and mystical commentaries; then will it be seen how the word-for-word meaning practically never suffices by itself and how apparent naiveties, inconsistencies, and contradictions resolve themselves in a dimension of profundity for which one must possess the key. The literal meaning is frequently a cryptic language that more often veils than reveals and that is only meant to furnish clues to truths of a cosmological, metaphysical, and mystical order; the Oriental traditions are unanimous concerning this complex and multidimensional interpretation of sacred texts. According to Meister Eckhart, the Holy Spirit teaches all truth; admittedly, there is a literal meaning that the author had in mind, but as God is the author of Holy Scripture, every true meaning is at the same time a literal meaning; for all that is true comes from the Truth itself, is contained in it, springs from it, and is willed by it. And so with Dante in his *Convivio:* "The Scriptures can be understood, and ought to be explained, principally in four senses. One is called literal. . . . The second is called allegorical. . . . The third sense is called moral. . . . The fourth sense is called anagogical, that is, beyond sense (*sovrasenso*); and this is when a Scripture is spiritually expounded, which, while true in its literal sense, refers beyond it to the higher things of the eternal

Glory, as we may see in that Psalm of the Prophet, where he says that when Israel went out of Egypt, Judea became holy and free. Which, although manifestly true according to the letter, is nonetheless true in its spiritual meaning, namely, that the soul, in forsaking its sins, is made holy and free in its powers" (*Trattato Secondo*, I).

As regards Biblical style—setting aside certain variations that are of no importance here—it is important to understand that the sacred or supra-human character of the text could never be manifested in an absolute way through language, which perforce is human; the divine quality referred to appears rather through the wealth of superposed meanings and in the theurgic power of the text when it is thought and pronounced and written.

Equally important is the fact that the Scriptures are sacred, not because of their subject matter and the way in which it is dealt with, but because of their degree of inspiration, or what amounts to the same, their divine origin; it is this that determines the contents of the book, and not the reverse. The Bible can speak of a multitude of things other than God without being the less sacred for it, whereas other books can deal with God and exalted matters and still not be the divine Word.

The apparent incoherence in certain sacred texts results ultimately from the disproportion between divine Truth and human language: it is as if this language, under the pressure of the Infinite, were shattered into a thousand disparate pieces or as if God had at His disposal no more than a few words to express a thousand truths, thus obliging Him to use all sorts of ellipses and paraphrases. According to the Rabbis, "God speaks succinctly"; this also explains the syntheses in sacred language that are incomprehensible *a priori*, as well as the superposition of meanings already mentioned. The role of the orthodox and inspired commentators is to intercalate in sentences, when too elliptic, the implied and unexpressed clauses, or to indicate in what way or in what sense a certain statement should be taken, besides explaining the different symbolisms, and so forth. It is the orthodox commentary and not the word-for-word meaning of the Torah that acts as law. The Torah is said to be "closed", and the sages "open" it; and it is precisely this "closed" nature of the Torah that renders necessary from the start the Mishnah, the commentary that was given in the tabernacle when Joshua transmitted it to the Sanhedrin. It is also said that God gave the Torah during the day and the Mishnah during the night and that the Torah is infinite in itself, whereas the Mishnah is inexhaustible as it flows forth in duration. It should also be noted that there are two principal degrees of inspiration, or even three if the orthodox commentaries are included; Judaism expresses the difference between the first two degrees by comparing the inspiration of Moses to a bright mirror and that of the other prophets to a dark mirror.

The two keys to the Bible are, as already stated, the ideas of symbolism and revelation. Too often revelation has been approached in a psychological, hence purely naturalistic and relativistic, sense. In reality revelation is the fulgurant irruption of a knowledge that comes, not from an individual or collective subconscious, but on the contrary from a supra-consciousness, which though latent in all beings nonetheless immensely surpasses its individual and psychological crystallizations. In saying that "the kingdom of God is within you", Jesus Christ means not that Heaven—or God—is of a psychological order, but simply that access to spiritual and divine realities is to be found at the center of our being, and it is from this center precisely that revelation springs forth when the human ambience offers a sufficient reason for it to do so and when therefore a predestined human vehicle presents itself, namely, one capable of conveying this outflow.

But clearly the most important basis for what we have just spoken of is the admission that a world of intelligible light exists, both underlying and transcending our consciousness; the knowledge of this world, or this sphere, entails as a consequence the negation of all psychologism and likewise all evolutionism. In other words, psychologism and evolutionism are nothing but makeshift hypotheses to compensate for the absence of this knowledge.

To affirm then that the Bible is both symbolistic and revealed means, on the one hand, that it expresses complex truths in a language that is indirect and full of imagery and, on the other, that its source is neither the sensorial world nor the psychological or rational plane, but rather a sphere of reality that transcends these planes and immensely envelops them, while yet in principle being accessible to man through the intellective and mystical center of his being, or through the "heart", if one prefers, or pure "Intellect". It is the Intellect which comprises in its very substance the evidence for the sphere of reality that we are speaking of and which thus contains the proof of it, if this word can have a meaning in the domain of direct and participative perception. Indeed the classic prejudice of scientism, or the fault in its method if one wishes, is to deny any mode of knowledge that is supra-sensorial and supra-rational, and in consequence to deny the planes of reality to which these modes refer and which constitute, precisely, the sources both of revelation and of intellection. Intellection—in principle—is for man what revelation is for the collectivity; in principle, we say, for in fact man cannot have access to direct intellection—or *gnosis*—except by virtue of a pre-existing scriptural revelation. What the Bible describes as the fall of man or the loss of Paradise coincides with our separation from total intelligence; this is why it is said that "the kingdom of God is within you", and again: "Knock, and it shall be opened unto you." The Bible itself is the multiple and mysterious objectification of this universal Intellect or *Logos*: it is thus the projection, by way of images and enigmas, of what we carry in a quasi-inaccessible depth at the bottom of our heart; and the facts of sacred history—where nothing is left to chance—are themselves cosmic projections of the unfathomable divine Truth.

Religio Perennis

One of the keys to understanding our true nature and our ultimate destiny is the fact that the things of this world are never proportionate to the actual range of our intelligence. Our intelligence is made for the Absolute, or else it is nothing; among all the intelligences of this world the human spirit alone is capable of objectivity, and this implies—or proves—that the Absolute alone confers on our intelligence the power to accomplish to the full what it can accomplish and to be wholly what it is.[1] If it were necessary or useful to prove the Absolute, the objective and transpersonal character of the human Intellect would be a sufficient testimony, for this Intellect is the indisputable sign of a purely spiritual first Cause, a Unity infinitely central but containing all things, an Essence at once immanent and transcendent. It has been said more than once that total Truth is inscribed in an eternal script in the very substance of our spirit; what the different Revelations do is to "crystallize" and "actualize", in different degrees according to the case, a nucleus of certitudes that not only abides forever in the divine Omniscience, but also sleeps by refraction in the "naturally supernatural" kernel of the individual, as well as in that of each ethnic or historical collectivity or the human species as a whole.

Similarly, in the case of the will, which is no more than a prolongation or complement of the intelligence: the objects it commonly sets out to achieve, or those that life imposes on it, do not measure up to the fullness of its range; only the "divine dimension" can satisfy the thirst for plenitude in our willing or our love. What makes our will human, and therefore free, is the fact that it is proportioned to God; in God alone it is kept free from all constraint, hence from everything that limits its nature.

The essential function of human intelligence is discernment between the Real and the illusory or between the Permanent and the impermanent, and the essential function of the will is attach-

---

[1] "Heaven and earth cannot contain Me (Allah), but the heart of My faithful servant containeth Me" (*hadîth qudsî*). Similarly Dante: "I perceive that our intellect is never satisfied if the True does not enlighten it, outside which no truth is possible" (*Paradiso* 4:124-26).

ment to the Permanent or the Real. This discernment and this attachment are the quintessence of all spirituality; carried to their highest level or reduced to their purest substance, they constitute the underlying universality in every great spiritual patrimony of humanity, or what may be called the *religio perennis*;[2] this is the religion to which the sages adhere, one which is always and necessarily founded upon formal elements of divine institution.[3]

*   *   *

Metaphysical discernment is a "separation" between *Âtmâ* and *Mâyâ*; contemplative concentration or unifying consciousness is on the contrary a "union" of *Mâyâ* with *Âtmâ*. Discernment is separative,[4] and it is what "doctrine" refers to; concentration is unitive, and it is what "method" refers to; "faith" is connected to the first element and "love of God" to the second.

To paraphrase the well-known saying of Saint Irenaeus, the *religio perennis* is fundamentally this: the Real entered into the illusory so that the illusory might be able to return into the Real. It is this mystery, together with the metaphysical discernment and contemplative concentration that are its complement, which alone is important in an absolute sense from the point of view of *gnosis*; for the gnostic—in the etymological and rightful sense of that word—there is in the last analysis no other "religion". It is what Ibn Arabi called the "religion of Love", placing the accent on the element "realization".

---

[2] These words recall the *philosophia perennis* of Steuchus Eugubin (sixteenth century) and the neo-scholastics; but the word *philosophia* suggests rightly or wrongly a mental elaboration rather than wisdom and therefore does not convey exactly the sense we intend. *Religio* is what "binds" man to Heaven and engages his whole being; as for the word *traditio*, it is related to a more outward and sometimes fragmentary reality, besides suggesting a retrospective outlook; a new-born religion "binds" men to Heaven from the moment of its first revelation, but it does not become a "tradition"—or have "traditions"—until two or three generations later.

[3] This is true even in the case of the pre-Islamic Arab sages, who lived spiritually on the heritage of Abraham and Ishmael.

[4] This is what the Arabic word *furqân* signifies, namely, "qualitative differentiation", from *faraqa*, to separate, discern, bifurcate; it is well known that *Furqân* is one of the names of the Koran.

Religio Perennis

The two-fold definition of the *religio perennis*—discernment between the Real and the illusory and a unifying and permanent concentration on the Real—implies in addition the criteria of intrinsic orthodoxy for every religion and all spirituality; in order to be orthodox a religion must possess a mythological or doctrinal symbolism establishing the essential distinction in question, and it must provide a path that guarantees both the perfection of concentration and its continuity; in other words a religion is orthodox if it provides a sufficient, if not always exhaustive, idea of the Absolute and the relative, and thus of their reciprocal relationships, and a spiritual activity that is contemplative in its nature and effectual with regard to our ultimate destiny. For it is notorious that heterodoxies always tend to adulterate either the idea of the divine Principle or the manner of our attachment to it; they offer a worldly, profane, or—if one prefers—"humanist" counterfeit of religion, or else a mysticism containing nothing but the ego and its illusions.

*   *   *

It may seem disproportionate to treat in simple and as it were schematic terms a subject as complex as that of spiritual perspectives, but since the very nature of things allows us to take into consideration an aspect of simplicity, the truth would be no better served by following the meanders of a complexity not called for in this case. Analysis is one function of the intelligence, and synthesis is another; the common association of intelligence with difficulty and ease with presumption obviously has no relation to the true nature of the Intellect. It is the same with intellectual vision as it is with optical vision: there are things which must be examined in detail if they are to be understood and others which are better seen from a certain distance and which, appearing simple, convey their real nature all the more clearly. Truth can expand and differentiate indefinitely, but it is also contained in a "geometrical point"; grasping this point is everything, whatever the symbol—or symbolism—that in fact brings about intellection.

Truth is one, and it would be vain to refuse to look for it except in one particular place, for the Intellect contains in its substance all that is true, and truth cannot but be manifested wherever the Intellect is deployed in the atmosphere of a Revelation. Space can be represented by a circle as well as by a cross, a spiral, a star, or a square; and just as it is impossible for there to be only one figure to represent the nature of space or extension, so it is also impossible for there to be only one doctrine giving an account of the Absolute and of the relations between the contingent and the Absolute; in other words, believing that there can be only one true doctrine is like denying the plurality of the geometrical figures used to indicate the characteristics of space or—to choose a very different example—the plurality of individual consciousnesses and visual points of view. In each Revelation, God says "I" while placing Himself extrinsically at a point of view other than that of earlier Revelations, hence the appearance of contradiction on the plane of formal crystallization.

The objection might be raised that the various geometrical figures are not strictly equivalent in their capacity to serve as adequations between graphic symbolism and spatial extension and thus that the comparison just made could also be used as an argument against the equivalence of traditional perspectives; to this we reply that traditional perspectives are not meant so much to be absolute adequations—at least *a priori*—as to be paths of salvation and means of deliverance. Besides, though the circle—not even to mention the point—is a more direct adequation of form to space than is the cross or any other differentiated figure, and though it therefore reflects more perfectly the nature of extension, there is still this to be considered: the cross, the square, or the spiral expresses explicitly a spatial reality that the circle or the point expresses only implicitly; the differentiated figures are therefore irreplaceable—otherwise they would not exist—and they are in no sense various kinds of imperfect circles; the cross is infinitely nearer the perfection of the point or the circle than is the oval or trapezoid, for example. Analogous considerations apply to traditional doctrines as regards their differences of form and their merits as an equation.

*　　*　　*

Let us return to our *religio perennis*, considered either as metaphysical discernment and unifying concentration or as the descent of the divine Principle, which becomes manifestation in order that manifestation may return to the Principle.

In Christianity—according to Saint Irenaeus and others—God "became man" that man might "become God"; in Hindu terms one would say: *Âtmâ* became *Mâyâ* that *Mâyâ* might become *Âtmâ*. In Christianity, contemplative and unifying concentration is to dwell in the manifested Real—the "Word made flesh"—in order that this Real might dwell in us, who are illusory, according to what Christ said in a vision granted to Saint Catherine of Siena: "I am He who is; thou art she who is not." The soul dwells in the Real—in the kingdom of God that is "within us"—by means of permanent prayer of the heart, as is taught by the parable of the unjust judge and the injunction of Saint Paul.

In Islam the same fundamental theme—fundamental because it is universal—is crystallized according to a very different perspective. Discernment between the Real and the non-real is affirmed by the Testimony of Unity (the *Shahâdah*): the correlative concentration on the Symbol or permanent consciousness of the Real is effected by this same Testimony or by the divine Name which synthesizes it and which is thus the quintessential crystallization of the Koranic Revelation; this Testimony or this Name is also the quintessence of the Abrahamic Revelation—through the lineage of Ishmael—and goes back to the primordial Revelation of the Semitic branch. The Real "descended" (*nazzala, unzila*); it entered into the non-real or illusory, the "perishable" (*fânin*)[5], in becoming the Koran—or the *Shahâdah* that summarizes it, or the *Ism* (the "Name") that is its sonorous and graphic essence, or the *Dhikr* (the "Mention") that is its operative synthesis—in order that upon this divine barque the illusory might return to the Real, to the "Face (*Wajh*) of the Lord that alone abides" (*wa yabqâ Wajhu Rabbika*),[6] whatever the metaphysical import attributed to the ideas of "illusion" and of "Reality". In this reciprocity lies all the mystery of the "Night of Destiny" (*Laylat al-Qadr*), which is a "descent", and of the "Night of Ascension" (*Laylat al-Mi'râj*), which is the complementary phase; contemplative realization—or "unification" (*tawhîd*)—partakes of this ascension of the Prophet through the degrees of Paradise. "Verily"—says the Koran—"prayer guards against the major (*fahshâ*) and the minor (*munkar*) sins, but the mention (*dhikr*) of *Allâh* is greater".[7]

---

[5] The word *fanâ'*, sometimes translated as "extinction" by analogy with the Sanskrit *nirvâna*, has the same root and literally means "perishable nature".

[6] *Sûrah* "The Merciful" [55]:27.

[7] *Sûrah* "The Spider" [29]:45.

Nearer to the Christian perspective in a certain connection, but much more remote in another, is the Buddhist perspective, which on the one hand is based on a "Word made flesh", but on the other hand knows nothing of the anthropomorphic notion of a creator God. In Buddhism the two terms of the alternative or of discernment are *Nirvâna*, the Real, and *Samsâra*, the illusory; in the last analysis the path is the permanent consciousness of *Nirvâna* as *Shûnya*, the "Void", or else it is concentration on the saving manifestation of *Nirvâna*, the Buddha, who is *Shûnyamûrti*, "Manifestation of the Void". In the Buddha—notably in his form Amitabha—*Nirvâna* became *Samsâra* that *Samsâra* might become *Nirvâna*; and if *Nirvâna* is the Real and *Samsâra* is illusion, the Buddha is the Real in the illusory, and the *Bodhisattva* is the illusory in the Real,[8] which suggests the symbolism of the *Yin-Yang*. The passage from the illusory to the Real is described in the *Prajnâpâramitâ-hridaya-sûtra* in these terms: "Gone, gone—gone for the other shore, attained the other shore, O Enlightenment, be blessed!"

*   *   *

It is in the nature of things that every spiritual outlook must place a conception of man in contrast with a corresponding conception of God; hence there arise three ideas or definitions: first, of man himself; second, of God as He reveals Himself to a man who is defined in this way; and third, of man as determined and transformed by God as a result of the outlook in question.

From the point of view of human subjectivity, man is the container, and God is the contained; from the divine point of view—if one can express it this way—the relationship is reversed, all things being contained in God and nothing being able to contain Him. To say that man is made in the image of God means at the same time that God assumes something of that image *a posteriori* and in connection with man; God is pure Spirit, and man is consequently intelligence or consciousness; conversely, if man is defined as intelligence, God appears as "Truth". In other words God, desiring

---

[8] See "Le mystère du Bodhisattva" (*Études Traditionnelles*, May-June, July-August, September-October, 1962). [Translator's note: For an English translation of this article, see "Mystery of the Bodhisattva" in *Treasures of Buddhism* (Bloomington, Indiana: World Wisdom Books, 1993), pp. 107-34.]

to affirm Himself under the aspect of "Truth", addresses Himself to man insofar as man is endowed with intelligence, just as He addresses Himself to man in distress to affirm His Mercy or to man endowed with free will to affirm Himself as the saving Law.

The "proofs" of God and religion are in man himself: "Knowing his own nature, he also knows Heaven," says Mencius, in agreement with other analogous and well-known maxims. We must extract from the givens of our own nature the key-certainty that opens up the way to certainty of the Divine and Revelation; to speak of "man" is to speak implicitly of "God"; to speak of the "relative" is to speak of the "Absolute". Human nature in general and human intelligence in particular cannot be understood apart from the religious phenomenon, which characterizes them in the most direct and most complete way possible: grasping the transcendent—not the "psychological"—nature of the human being, we thereby grasp the nature of revelation, religion, tradition; we understand their possibility, their necessity, their truth. And in understanding religion, not only in a particular form or in a word-for-word way, but in its formless essence, we also understand the religions, that is to say, the meaning of their plurality and diversity; this is the plane of *gnosis*, of the *religio perennis*, where the extrinsic antinomies of dogma are explained and resolved.

*　　*　　*

On the outward and therefore contingent plane—which nonetheless has its importance in the human order—there is a concordance between the *religio perennis* and virgin nature and by the same token between it and primordial nudity, that of creation, birth, resurrection, or the high priest in the Holy of Holies, a hermit in the desert,[9] a Hindu *sâdhu* or *sannyâsin*, a Red Indian in silent prayer on a mountain.[10] Nature inviolate is at once a vestige of the earthly

---

[9] Such as Mary of Egypt, in whose case the non-formal and wholly inward character of a love effected by God partakes of the qualities of *gnosis*, so much so that one could call it a "*gnosis* of love" in the sense of *parabhakti*.

[10] Simplicity of clothing and its color, white in particular, sometimes replace the symbolism of nudity within the framework of sartorial art; on every plane the laying bare that is inspired by the naked Truth counterbalances a worldly "culturism". In other connections, however, a sacred robe symbolizes the victory of the Spirit over

Paradise and a prefiguration of the heavenly Paradise; sanctuaries and garments differ, but virgin nature and the human body remain faithful to the initial unity. Sacred art, which seems to move away from that unity, in reality simply serves to restore to natural phenomena their divine messages, to which men have become insensitive; in art, the perspective of love tends toward overflowing and profusion whereas the perspective of *gnosis* tends toward nature, simplicity, and silence; such is the contrast between Gothic richness and Zen sobriety.[11] But this must not lead us to lose sight of the fact that outward frameworks or modes are always contingent and that all combinations and all compensations are possible, especially since in spirituality every possibility can be reflected in every other according to the appropriate modalities.

A civilization is integral and healthy to the extent it is founded on the "invisible" or "underlying" religion, the *religio perennis*, that is, to the extent its expressions or forms are transparent to the Non-Formal and tend toward the Origin, thus conveying the recollection of a lost Paradise, but also—and with all the more reason—the presentiment of a timeless Beatitude. For the Origin is at once within us and before us; time is but a spiral movement around a motionless Center.

---

the flesh, and its hieratic richness—which we are far from criticizing—expresses the inexhaustible profusion of Mystery and Glory.

[11] But it is very apparent that the most sumptuous sacred art is infinitely nearer to *gnosis* than the ignorant and affected "sparingness" of those of our contemporaries who profess to be "making a clean sweep". Only a simplicity that is qualitative, noble, and conformable to the essence of things reflects and transmits the perfume of non-formal wisdom.

Appendix

The selections on the following pages have been taken from the author's previously unpublished notes and correspondence. In addition to the many articles he wrote for publication, Schuon composed throughout his life numerous brief texts that were available only privately and to a small number of readers. He also wrote hundreds of letters, often in response to spiritual questions from people whom he was never to meet as well as from those he knew well. Without being at all systematic in approach, the selections presented here are intended to illustrate, emphasize, or shed additional light upon some of the key ideas found in the preceding chapters.

*　　　*　　　*

We say that there is an absolute, transcendent Reality, not perceivable by the senses, beyond space and time, but knowable by the pure Intellect, through which it makes itself present, a Reality which, without ever undergoing the slightest change since it is unconditional, gives rise—by reason of its very Infinitude—to a dimension of contingency or relativity so as to be able to actualize the mystery of its radiation. For "it is in the nature of the Good to wish to communicate itself": in other words, God wishes to be known not only within Himself, but also "from without" and from the standpoint of "another than Himself"; this is the very substance of the divine All-Possibility.

This is what we say, or remind of, *a priori*. We do not say it only because we believe it, but because we know it, and we know it because we are it. We are it in our transpersonal Intellect, which intrinsically conveys the immanent presence of the absolute Reality and without which we would not be human beings.

*　　　*　　　*

Religion—*religio*—is what "binds" us to Heaven; the modes or forms may vary, but the principle remains invariable. All religion comprises a doctrine and a method; the method includes the ritual, moral, and social elements, and the doctrine the dogmatic elements, without there always being a clear separation between the two orders.

All religion comprises essentially metaphysical discernment between the Real and the illusory, on the one hand, and permanent concentration on the Real, on the other; this discernment is the essence of all doctrine, and this concentration is the essence of all method. To say that the religions comprise these two elements "essentially", hence by definition, is to say that there is an "essential religion", a *religio perennis*.

The *religio perennis* is in fact underlying in relation to the diverse religions; it cannot live *de facto* outside them and is therefore contained within the diverse esoterisms, or it constitutes them, according to the case. One must not lose sight of the fact that the majority of esoterisms have an exoterizing aspect, which in any case is identical more or less with the bhaktic perspective. And we would add that many heresies are attempts—unconsciously and in error—to rediscover the *religio perennis*.

*   *   *

Man bears within himself all the gifts and means of a religion, but he no longer has access to them on account of the fall: whence, precisely, the necessity—relative, in principle—of outward forms, which awaken and actualize man's spiritual potentialities, but which also risk limiting them; whence in addition the necessity of esoterism.

The criterion of an authentic spirituality is not only the consciousness of the primacy of *Âtmâ* and the relativity of *Mâyâ* and then the practice of a method of realization and union combined with the sincere practice of the virtues, but also, as a formal condition, a valid attachment to an intrinsically orthodox religion. It is only thus that man presents himself as a "valid interlocutor" on the spiritual plane: first in relation to God, and then in relation to his fellow men.

The spiritual life, we repeat, is first our consciousness of the nature of God; then it is our relationship with God; and finally it is the conditions for this relationship, both moral and traditional; for spirituality requires not only the conformation of our character to the divine Norm, but also, extrinsically, our integration into a sacred system.

*   *   *

I must call your attention to an important aspect of universality, or unity: the divergence between religions is not only due to the incomprehension of men; it is also within the Revelations, hence in the divine Will, and that is why there is a difference between exoterism and esoterism; the diverse dogmas contradict each other, not only in the minds of theologians, but also—and *a priori*—in the Sacred Scriptures; but God, in giving these Scriptures, at the same time gives the keys for understanding their underlying unity. If all men were metaphysicians and contemplatives, a single Revelation might be enough; but since this is not so, the Absolute must reveal itself in different ways, and the metaphysical viewpoints from which these Revelations are derived—in keeping with different needs for causal explanations and different spiritual temperaments—cannot but contradict one another on the plane of forms, somewhat as geometrical figures contradict one another as long as one has not grasped their spatial and symbolic homogeneity. God could not wish that everyone understand Unity, since this understanding is contrary to the nature of man in the "dark age". This is why I am against ecumenism, which is an impossibility and an absurdity pure and simple. The great evil is not that men of different religions do not understand each other, but that too many men—due to the influence of the modern spirit—are no longer believers. If religious divergences are becoming particularly painful in our time, this is uniquely because the divisions between believers have become all the more acute, and also all the more dangerous, in the face of the unbelief that has become more and more menacing. It is therefore urgent: 1. that men return to faith, whatever their religion may be—on condition that it is intrinsically orthodox—and in spite of dogmatic ostracisms; 2. that those who are capable of understanding pure metaphysics, esoterism, and the internal unity of religions discover these truths and draw the necessary inward and outward conclusions.

*   *   *

The first constitutive element of the *religio perennis* is metaphysical discernment, the methodical support of which is meditation. It contains all truth, all knowledge, all certitude.

The second element is mystical concentration, the support of which is perpetual and quintessential orison. It contains all spiritual practice.

These two elements would remain ineffectual, or even become harmful, without the concurrence of a third: namely, moral conformity, beauty of character, nobility of sentiments and of comportment; for the path encompasses all that we are. "Every house divided against itself shall not stand." One must be what one knows and what one wants to become, a paradoxical formulation but one full of meaning.

The general conditions of our earthly world are such that these three elements, to be able to bear their fruits and to be sheltered from all deviation, need a framework of traditional orthodoxy, hence a religion; without this, wisdom would disappear; the path would enjoy no guarantee of authenticity.

Finally, there is the question of ambience, of formal surroundings: this element is integral liturgy. Our formal ambience must be in conformity with our inner life, whence the rules of sacred art and traditional art—or craftsmanship—in general; no material object escapes these disciplines: symbolism and beauty; mathematical and musical qualities. "God is beautiful, and He loveth beauty."

*   *   *

Our ambience—as well as our personality—inevitably pertains to the particular, not the Universal; to possible being, not Necessary Being; to the relative good, not the Sovereign Good.

There is thus no reason to be troubled because one lives in this particular ambience rather than another; living in space and time, one clearly has to be situated somewhere at a certain moment. And there is likewise no reason to be troubled because one is this person rather than someone else; being a person—on pain of non-existence—one has indeed to be a particular person, that is, such-and-such a person and not the person as such; or rather the person as such in such-and-such a person.

What matters is to maintain, and to strengthen, our contact with the Universal, the life-giving, stabilizing, sanctifying, and saving essence of our particularity; with Necessary Being, the essence of our possible existence; with the Sovereign Good, the essence of our relative qualities. The Absolute is the essence of positive contingency, or of the contingent insofar as it is positive in itself.

* * *

It is true that metaphysical truth by definition transcends all forms, hence all religions; but man is a form, and he cannot attain to the non-formal except in a form; otherwise the religions would not exist. The religious form must be transcended within religion itself, in its esoterism. "Without me ye can do nothing," Christ said, and he knew whereof he spoke. And Muhammad said, "None shall meet Allah who hath not first met His Prophet."

Spiritual seeking must start with the following truths-principles. First of all, metaphysical truth is essentially the discernment between the Real and the illusory: *Âtmâ* and *Mâyâ*, *Nirvâna* and *Samsâra*, God and the world; all relative truths are derived from this fundamental discernment, which is to be found in the esoterism of every intrinsically orthodox religion. Second, this truth requires quasi-perpetual concentration on the Real. In Hesychasm, this is the function of the "Jesus Prayer" or "Prayer of the Heart"; it is the "remembrance of Allah", *japa-yoga*, the *nembutsu*. Third, there is the practice of the virtues, which are essential, for "vertical" realization requires "horizontal" perfection; it also requires, apart from the moral virtues, the qualities of dignity and nobility. Fourth, all of this is situated in the framework of a traditional orthodoxy, with all of its liturgical conditions; and sacred art, in the broadest sense, is part of those conditions.

* * *

It happens that ascetics disparage beauty and aspire to the "destruction of the ego"—at least in their language, for such a thing is useless in principle and impossible in fact; if they express themselves in this way, it is because they place themselves at the point of view of desire and attachment, hence of the passional soul; they give an over-accentuated example without representing the norm. Now the human norm is to be *pontifex*; it is to realize equilibrium between two poles of attraction; it is to connect two shores, the inner and the outer.

Man is situated between the inner and the outer just as the *Logos* is situated between God and the world, and as Being is situated between Beyond-Being and Existence: hence between the Essence and the *Logos*.

On the one hand, to contemplate God in the inward and to recognize His reflections in the outward; on the other hand, to manifest Him in the outward while launching oneself toward Him in the inward.

When the inner dimension takes precedence over the outer, man will no longer undergo the tyranny of phenomena, but at the same time he will see them with the eye of inwardness: positive phenomena will be for him messengers of the inward and factors of interiorization. When one knows that beauty comes from the inward and bears witness to the inward, one will seek it in the inward. "The kingdom of God is within you."

*   *   *

Man is by definition a *pontifex*, a "builder of bridges"—or "a bridge". For man possesses essentially two dimensions, an outward and an inward; he therefore has the right to both, or else he would not be man, precisely; to speak of a man without surroundings is as contradictory as to speak of a man without a core. On the one hand, we live in phenomena which surround us and of which we are a part, and on the other hand, our hearts are rooted in God; consequently we must realize as perfect an equilibrium as possible between our life in the world and our life directed toward the Divine. Obviously this second life determines the first and gives it all its meaning; the rights of outwardness depend upon measures which pertain to the inward and which the inward imposes upon us.

Worldliness exteriorizes the inward; spirituality interiorizes the outward; that is, it discerns in the outward the archetypes, which by their essentiality are interiorizing. Profane men "carnalize" the spirit, if one may put it thus, whereas spiritual men—the "twice-born"—spiritualize the "flesh"; they spiritualize it in respect of the metaphysical transparency of phenomena, while excluding it in respect of pure and simple materiality, which coincides with passionality.

This is the mystery of compensatory complementarity (= *Yin-Yang*), in relation to which the spiritual "yes" must include a "no", and the spiritual "no", a "yes".

* * *

As for the environment which surrounds us and with which we surround ourselves, it is important because form is important; for we live among forms and we are a form, a form "made in the image of God". To affirm that "the spirit alone counts" is a hypocritical and unrealistic "angelism"—as if matter did not exist and as if an existing and ubiquitous thing could have no spiritual significance whatever. This is a typically profane error and thus as far removed as possible from esoterism, which insists not only on the symbolism of things—in art or handicrafts as well as in nature—but also on their aesthetic, moral, and quasi-musical message. The environment is an indirect element of intelligence and beauty in the spiritual life.

* * *

When the imagination is cured of its worldliness and egoism, it can rest calmly in prayer. The devil hates this calm and seeks to destroy it by causing all sorts of troubles, and he is greatly helped in this by the worldly hypnosis to which the imagination is subject.

The Intellect is active, being centered on the Truth; the soul is passive, imaginative, sentimental, passional, and ready to be distracted.

To be a hypocrite is to accept the Truth without the soul conforming and acting in consequence. To be sincere, on the contrary, is to conform to the Truth one adheres to and to act in keeping with this adherence.

It is not enough to know theoretically that "the next world is better for thee than this world"; it is also necessary to believe it. The intelligence can be full of lofty thoughts, of sublime truths, when the imaginative and feeling soul is far from being up to the level of these contents of the intelligence; and it is important to close this gap, which gives rise to pretentiousness and hypocrisy. The soul must be up to the level of the spirit.

* * *

The exoteric message of a religion addresses itself to an average ethnic mentality, taking account of its limitations and needs; this message nevertheless conveys teachings whose esoteric and universal bearing is understood by the gnostics, the "theosophers" in the proper sense of the word. Thus Christian esoterism is a perspective of inwardness: Christ intended that we should go to God "in spirit and in truth", and he objected to the "commandments of men", which is to say that sincerity of heart takes precedence over formalistic religion. "The kingdom of God is within you"; the Self is immanent; the Intellect, according to Meister Eckhart, is "uncreated". Jesus represents the Truth and the Way; Mary is the aspect of Beauty and Grace.

Those of us who are not of Oriental origin owe to Judaism—indirectly or directly—the concept of a personal God who is at once Creator and Lawgiver; the God of the Bible, the Ten Commandments, the Psalms. David shows us how to speak to God.

But there are not only the religions that find their expression through Books; there are also those based on the symbolisms of virgin Nature; Hinduism combines the two modes. Let us specify that the so-called primitive religions are of very unequal levels, but some of them have retained a sufficient efficacy, such as Far Eastern Shamanism and certain traditions of the American Indians. We must mention here Shinto—whose case is substantially similar—because the art and crafts of Japan have succeeded in introducing primordial simplicity into the elaborate art of the later periods; for the outward, far from being negligible, has its spiritual importance; "extremes meet". The spirit is opposed to exteriorizing formalism, but not to positive forms; on the contrary, it determines them and enters into them, and through them makes us live.

*   *   *

A heathen is a man who worships idols and ignores or rejects God; as for the American Indians, they never worshiped idols, nor did they ignore or reject God, the Great Spirit. Consequently, the Indians are not heathens, and their religion, though not fully understood by every individual Indian, is a true one, and God is working in it and gives His Grace in it.

One often reads in so-called "scientific" books that the word *Wakan Tanka* does not mean God, any more than other words in the Indian languages, such as *Wakonda, Tirawa, Natosiwa, Manitou, Yastasinan*; it is forgotten—or rather people are incapable of understanding—that the occidental idea of "God" concerns only the personal aspect of the Divinity and that the Indian names of the Great Spirit involve another aspect of the divine Reality. *Wakan Tanka* is not only God as personal Creator, but also God as impersonal Essence; He is not only God as pure Principle, but also as His own manifestation—or reflected power—within Creation, and even, in a certain sense, God as Creation, insofar as it is possible to speak in this way. *Wakan Tanka* means not only what is exclusively but also immanently God in the same manner that the Hindu word *Âtmâ* means not only the divine Reality but also everything insofar as it is considered a manifestation of the divine Reality. Though *Wakan Tanka* can be translated as "Mysterious Power" or otherwise, the expression "Great Spirit", which displeases many "scientists", is certainly the best, for it involves no restriction.

All Indian rites, such as the most holy pipe, or the sweat lodge, or fasting and calling to the Great Spirit in search of a vision or power or illumination, or the Sun Dance and other rites—all this has without any doubt its deep metaphysical meaning and therefore its spiritual efficacy. The essential part of every religion, besides the ritual transmission of a spiritual influence preserved and given by priests, is prayer or invocation of God's Name. This invocation of God, when bestowed in the proper ritual conditions by a traditional priest—a "medicine man" possessing the corresponding authority, function, or power—and when accomplished in a good manner, pronounced in the holy language with serious concentration of the mind, in the beginning with fasting, and above all with the trusting hope, faith, and certitude of being accepted by God and attaining to Him after death or even in this life: this invocation of God, the Great Spirit, is the very essence of every religion.

In addition to the invocation aloud there is a silent one; I have heard that the Indians often pray silently. This kind of mute prayer is practiced in Asia as well: the tongue keeps quiet, but the mind is strongly concentrated on the one divine Reality; man is silent like the sky, not thinking with the head, but contemplating the Great Mystery with the heart, and empty of all earthly things.

In His Name, God is really present; and therefore our heart, when invoking Him, must be present too. Then He purifies us by the grace of His Name; He gives us perfections we did not have before; and finally He leads us back to Himself.

* * *

Easterners often underestimate the danger that lies in modern science. This science is in fact vitiated at its very core by two main misconceptions: "evolutionism" and "psychology". For a traditional mind, it is not difficult to see that the idea of evolution must be false, since the origin of a spiritual form is always better than its end. Without the preceding corruption of the "latter days", Lord Maitreya cannot come. Europe was spiritually healthy in the so-called "dark" Middle Ages, whereas it is our present age that is dark. As to the "psychologism" of modern universities, its error consists in reducing the spiritual to the psychological and in believing there is nothing beyond the realm of psychology—in other words, that this very limited science can attain to all inner realities, which is absurd. This view would imply that psychology, or even psychoanalysis, could comprehend *Satori* or *Nirvâna*. Modern science, like modern civilization as a whole, is thoroughly profane, having lost all sense of the sacred, reducing everything to merely individual and trivial dimensions. Everything is "humanized", hence the concept of "humanism". The notion of the spiritual is entirely lacking; every phenomenon is reduced to mere "natural" causes. Sacred and traditional wisdom is put on the same level as profane and individualistic "philosophy". Modern science has discovered a large number of facts, but it has forgotten and ridiculed those truths without which life has no value at all. Moreover, what modern science gives with one hand, it takes away with the other, for the wonders of surgery necessarily go together with those of nuclear bombs. In Europe and America, and in the modern world in general, people frequently desire spirituality without tradition, which is an entirely false attitude, since the first condition of a serious spiritual development is the restoration of a traditional mind. Westerners want to "try" everything instead of beginning on the basis of metaphysical certainty. Truth is beauty, and beauty comes only through tradition. We cannot change the world, but we can remain conscious of the truth, which is timeless. I write all this to let you know our position. It may be of interest to you, coming as it does from that very Europe which gave rise to the modern deviation.

Appendix

*   *   *

There is a mental, separative, discontinuous, indirect Knowledge, which is certitude and serenity; and there is a cardiac, unitive, continuous, direct Knowledge, which is identity and love.

Mental Knowledge comprises the relationship of subject and object, whereas cardiac Knowledge is subjective in the sense that the subject identifies itself with its object, or that it bears the object within itself; in this Knowledge there is neither objectification nor outwardness. It is for this reason that we can represent it by centripetal rays, that is, by a star, whereas the image of mental or objective Knowledge will be a system of concentric circles; in this case, there is analogy and not identity.

Mental Knowledge proceeds by comprehension; cardiac Knowledge by concentration. Truth and Love.

But there are not only the concentric circles and the star; there is also the spiral: this means that mental Knowledge participates in cardiac Knowledge to the extent it prolongs it, that is, to the extent it possesses a contemplative, hence interiorizing, quality.

The contingent cannot reach the Absolute; thought cannot enter into Reality to the point of merging itself in it. But the Absolute can enter the contingent; God can enter into the heart.

*   *   *

God has opened a gate in the middle of creation, and this open gate of the world toward God is man; this opening is God's invitation to look toward Him, to tend toward Him, to persevere with regard to Him, and to return to Him. And this enables us to understand why the gate shuts at death when it has been scorned during life; for to be man means nothing other than to look beyond and to pass through the gate. Unbelief and paganism are whatever turns its back on the gate; on its threshold light and darkness separate. The notion of hell becomes perfectly clear when we think how senseless it is—and what a waste and suicide—to slip through the human state without being truly man, that is, to pass God by, and thus to pass our own souls by, as if we had any right to human faculties apart from the return to God, and as if there were any point in the miracle of the human state apart from the end which is prefigured in man himself; or again: as if God had had no motive in giving us an intelligence that discerns and a will that chooses.

Granted that this gate is a center—and it must be one since it leads to God—it corresponds to a rare and precious possibility, and one that is unique for its surroundings. And this explains why there is damnation; for he who has refused to pass through the gate will never afterward be able to cross its threshold. Hence the representation of the afterlife as an implacable alternative: seen from the gate—that is, from the human state—there is no choice other than between the inside and the outside.

*   *   *

The divine Substance is comparable to water; accidents—cosmic phenomena—are like waves, drops, snow, ice; phenomena of the world or phenomena of the soul.

The Substance is pure Power, pure Spirit, pure Felicity. Accidentality transcribes these dimensions in limitative, even privative, mode; on the one hand, it "is not", and on the other hand, it "is" the Substance.

Accidentality is the contingent subject and the contingent object; it is contingency, for the Substance alone is necessary Being. Accidentality is the world that surrounds us and the life that carries us along; it is the aspect—or the phase—of the object and the point of view—or the present—of the subject; it is our heredity, our character, our tendencies, our capacities, our destiny; the fact of being born in a given form, at a given place, at a given moment, and of undergoing given sensations, given influences, and given experiences. All this is accidentality, and all this is nothing; for all this is not necessary Being; all this is limited on the one hand and passing on the other. And in the final analysis the content of all this is Felicity; it is this that attracts us by a thousand reverberations and under a thousand disguises; it is this that we desire in all our passing fancies, without knowing it.

Therefore, one must hold fast to Felicity, which is none other than Substance, and the support of which is prayer.

Glossary of Foreign Terms and Phrases

Advaita (Sanskrit): "non-dualist" interpretation of the *Vedânta*; Hindu doctrine according to which the seeming multiplicity of things is regarded as the product of ignorance, the only true reality being *Brahma*, the One, the Absolute, the Infinite, which is the unchanging ground of appearance.

Agapê (Greek): selfless "love", as of God for man and man for God; human compassion for one's neighbor; equivalent of Latin *caritas*.

Âkhir (Arabic): the "Last"; in Islam, *al-Âkhir* is a divine Name, as in the Koranic verse, "He is the First and the Last, the Outward and the Inward" (*Sûrah* "Iron" [57]:3).

Apocatastasis (Greek): "restitution, restoration"; among certain Christian theologians, including Clement of Alexandria, Origen, and Gregory of Nyssa, the doctrine that all creatures will finally be saved.

Âtmâ or *Âtman* (Sanskrit): the real or true "Self", underlying the ego and its manifestations; in the perspective of *Advaita Vedânta*, identical with *Brahma*.

Avatâra (Sanskrit): the earthly "descent", incarnation, or manifestation of God, especially of Vishnu in the Hindu tradition.

Awwal (Arabic): the "First"; in Islam, *al-Awwal* is a divine Name, as in the Koranic verse, "He is the First and the Last, the Outward and the Inward" (*Sûrah* "Iron" [57]:3).

Barakah (Arabic): "blessing", grace; in Islam, a spiritual influence or energy emanating originally from God, but often attached to sacred objects and spiritual persons.

Bâtin (Arabic): the "Inward"; in Islam, *al-Bâtin* is a divine Name, as in the Koranic verse, "He is the First and the Last, the Outward and the Inward" (*Sûrah* "Iron" [57]:3); also used with the meaning "esoteric".

Bhakti or *bhakti mârga* (Sanskrit): the spiritual "path" (*mârga*) of "love" (*bhakti*) and devotion to God; a person following such a path is a *bhakta*; see *jnâna, karma,* and *mârga.*

Bodhisattva (Sanskrit, Pali): literally, "enlightenment-being"; in *Mahâyâna* Buddhism, one who postpones his own final enlightenment and entry into *Nirvâna* in order to aid all other sentient beings in their quest for Buddhahood.

Bön (Tibetan): the ancient, pre-Buddhist religion of Tibet, which still exists today; adherents are called *Bön-Pos.*

Brahma or *Brahman* (Sanskrit): in Hinduism, the impersonal Absolute or ultimate Reality; to be distinguished from *Brahmâ,* that is, God in the personal aspect of Creator.

Brâhmana (Sanskrit): "Brahmin"; a member of the highest of the four Hindu castes; a priest or spiritual teacher; the distinctive quality of the *brâhmana* is his sacerdotal nature, tending toward wisdom and contemplativity; see *kshatriya, shûdra, vaishya.*

Caritas (Latin): selfless "love", as of God for man and man for God; human compassion for one's neighbor; equivalent of Greek *agapê.*

Corpus mysticum (Latin): literally, "mystical body"; one of the traditional epithets for the Christian Church, understood as the Body of Christ (*cf.* Eph. 4:4-13) and nourished by the Eucharist.

Creatio ex nihilo (Latin): "creation out of nothing"; the doctrine that God Himself is the sufficient cause of the universe, needing nothing else; often set in contrast to emanationist cosmogonies.

Dâr al-islâm (Arabic): literally, "abode of peace"; Muslim term for territories subject to Islam and Islamic religious law.

Deo volente (Latin): literally, "God willing", or "if God should so will".

Dhâkir (Arabic): "the one who invokes" or "remembers"; in Sufism, *dhâkir* usually means the human devotee who practices invocation as a spiritual method; it can also mean the supreme Self as the sole agent of consciousness; see *dhikr, Madhkûr*.

Dhikr (Arabic): "remembrance" of God, based upon the repeated invocation of His Name; central to Sufi practice, where the remembrance is often supported by the single word *Allâh*; see *dhâkir, Madhkûr*.

Ex divino (Latin): "from God"; used in connection with the doctrine of creation *ex nihilo*: God creates "out of nothing" but Himself, the universe thus proceeding "from God".

Ex nihilo (Latin): "out of nothing"; see *creatio ex nihilo*.

Ghâfilûn (Arabic, singular *ghâfil*): literally, "the heedless"; in Islam, *ghaflah* is the sin of indifference toward God.

Gnosis (Greek): "knowledge"; spiritual insight, principial comprehension, divine wisdom.

Guna (Sanskrit): literally, "strand"; quality, characteristic, attribute; in Hindu *Sânkhya*, the *guna*s are the three constituents of *Prakriti*: *sattva* (the ascending, luminous quality), *rajas* (the expansive, passional quality), and *tamas* (the descending, dark quality).

Guru (Sanskrit): literally, "weighty", grave, venerable; in Hinduism, a spiritual master; one who gives initiation and instruction in the spiritual path and in whom is embodied the supreme goal of realization or perfection.

Hadîth (Arabic, plural *ahâdîth*): "saying, narrative"; an account of the words or deeds of the Prophet Muhammad, transmitted through a traditional chain of known intermediaries; in a *hadîth qudsî* ("sacred saying"), Muslims consider that it is God Himself speaking.

Hamsa (Sanskrit): literally, "swan"; in Hinduism, the caste of primordial man, including all the positive attributes of the *brâhmana*, *kshatriya*, and *vaishya*.

Increatum et increabile (Latin): "uncreated and uncreatable"; transcending the domain of time and relativity, as the Absolute or its prolongations.

Îshvara (Sanskrit): one who "possesses power"; God understood as a personal being, as Creator and Lord; according to *Advaita Vedânta*, *Îshvara* is *Brahma* as conditioned by *Mâyâ*.

Japa-Yoga (Sanskrit): method of "union" or "unification" (*yoga*) based upon the "repetition" (*japa*) of a *mantra* or sacred formula, often containing one of the Names of God.

Jîvan-mukta (Sanskrit): one who is "liberated" while still in this "life"; a person who has attained a station of spiritual perfection or self-realization before death; in contrast to the *videha-mukta*, one who is liberated at the moment of death.

Jnâna or *jnâna mârga* (Sanskrit): the spiritual "path" (*mârga*) of sapiential "knowledge" (*jnâna*) or *gnosis*; a person following such a path is called a *jnânin*; see *bhakti*, *karma*, and *mârga*.

Kami (Japanese): in Shinto, the sacred, spiritual powers that animate all things; deities associated with eminent personages, sacred places, and the phenomena of nature.

Karma or *karma mârga* (Sanskrit): the spiritual "path" (*mârga*) of "action" (*karma*) or righteous deeds (see *bhakti* and *jnâna*); in Hinduism and Buddhism, *karma* is also the law of consequences, through which the present is explained by reference to the nature and quality of one's past actions.

Kshatriya (Sanskrit): a member of the second highest of the four Hindu castes; a warrior or prince; the distinctive quality of the *kshatriya* is a combative and noble nature that tends toward glory and heroism; see *brâhmana*, *sûdra*, *vaishya*

Laylat al-Mi'râj (Arabic): literally, "Night of the Ascent"; in Islam, the night in which the Prophet Muhammad was miraculously transported to Jerusalem before ascending to the divine Presence; in Sufism, the prototype of the highest station of mystical experience.

Laylat al-Qadr (Arabic): literally, "Night of Power"; the night in the year 610 A.D. during which the Koran descended in its entirety into the heart of the Prophet Muhammad.

Logos (Greek): "word, reason"; in Christian theology, the divine, uncreated Word of God (*cf.* John 1:1); the transcendent Principle of creation and revelation.

Madhkûr (Arabic): "the One invoked" or "remembered"; God, the Absolute; see *dhâkir, dhikr.*

Mahâpralaya (Sanskrit): in Hinduism, the "great" or final "dissolving" of the universe at the end of a *kalpa,* or "day in the life of *Brahmâ*", understood as lasting one thousand *yuga*s.

Mahâyâna (Sanskrit): literally, "great way"; with *Theravâda* ("way of the elders"), one of the two principal schools of Buddhism; distinguished by the idea that *Nirvâna* is not other than *Samsâra* truly seen as it is.

Mârga (Sanskrit): spiritual "way, path"; see *bhakti, jnâna, karma.*

Materia prima (Latin): "first or prime matter"; in Platonic cosmology, the undifferentiated and primordial substance serving as a "receptacle" for the shaping force of divine forms or ideas; universal potentiality.

Mâyâ (Sanskrit): "artifice, illusion"; in *Advaita Vedânta,* the beguiling concealment of *Brahma* in the form or under the appearance of a lower reality.

Natura naturans (Latin): literally, "nature naturing"; the active power that constitutes and governs the phenomena of the physical world.

Natura naturata (Latin): literally, "nature natured"; the phenomena of the physical world considered as the effect of an inward and invisible power.

Nembutsu (Japanese): "remembrance or mindfulness of the Buddha", based upon the repeated invocation of his Name; same as *buddhâ-nusmriti* in Sanskrit and *nien-fo* in Chinese.

Nirvâna (Sanskrit): "blowing out, extinction"; in Indian traditions, especially Buddhism, the extinction of the fires of passion and the resulting, supremely blissful state of liberation from attachment and egoism.

Nox profunda (Latin): literally, "deep night"; in the spiritual path, the experience of loss and darkness accompanying the death of the ego.

Panta rhei (Greek): literally, "everything flows"; the philosophy of the pre-Socratic philosopher Heraclitus (500 B.C.) that everything is constantly changing.

Parabhakti (Sanskrit): "supreme devotion"; Hinduism recognizes several degrees of *bhakti*, *parabhakti* being the highest.

Pax Romana (Latin): "Roman peace"; the law and order imposed by ancient Rome on its territories.

Perinde ac cadaver (Latin): literally, "in the manner of a corpse"; used in describing the submission of a disciple to a spiritual master.

Pontifex (Latin): "bridge-maker"; man as the link between Heaven and earth.

Prakriti (Sanskrit): literally, "making first" (see *materia prima*); the fundamental, "feminine" substance or material cause of all things; see *guna, Purusha*.

Pralaya (Sanskrit): "dissolution"; Hindu teaching that all appearance is subject to a periodic process of destruction and recreation; see *mahâpralaya*.

Purusha (Sanskrit): literally, "man"; the informing or shaping principle of creation; the "masculine" demiurge or fashioner of the universe; see *Prakriti*.

Quod absit (Latin): literally, "which is absent from, opposed to, or inconsistent with"; a phrase commonly used by the medieval scholastics to call attention to an idea that is absurdly inconsistent with accepted principles.

Sâdhu (Sanskrit): literally, one who is "accomplished, virtuous, holy"; a person living a life of asceticism, often withdrawn from the world.

Samsâra (Sanskrit): literally, "wandering"; in Hinduism and Buddhism, transmigration or the cycle of birth, death, and rebirth; also the world of apparent flux and change.

Sânkhya or *Sâmkhya* (Sanskrit): literally, "enumeration, calculation"; Hindu cosmological teaching in which nature is understood to result from the union of *Purusha* and *Prakriti*; one of the six orthodox *darshana*s, or perspectives, of classical Hinduism.

Sannyâsin (Sanskrit): "one who gives up or lays aside"; in Hinduism, a person who has entered upon the final stage of life, in which all worldly ties are abandoned; a wandering, mendicant monk.

Satori (Japanese): Zen term for the experience of enlightenment; spiritual realization.

Sattva (Sanskrit): in Hindu *Sânkhya*, the ascending, luminous *guna* or quality.

Shahâdah (Arabic): literally, "testimony, witness"; the fundamental doctrine of Islam, consisting of two statements or "testimonies": *lâ ilâha illâ 'Llâh*, "There is no god but [the one] God"; and *Muhammadun rasûlu 'Llâh*, "Muhammad is the messenger of God".

Shaykh (Arabic): literally, "old man, elder"; in Sufism, a spiritual master, comparable to a Hindu *guru*, whose authority is derived from submission to the discipline and instruction of a previous *shaykh* and thus from attachment to a traditional spiritual lineage.

Shûdra (Sanskrit): a member of the lowest of the four Hindu castes; the distinctive quality of the *shûdra* lies in his submission and fidelity to his superiors; see *brâhmana, kshatriya, vaishya.*

Shûnya (Sanskrit): "void", "emptiness"; in *Mahâyâna* Buddhism, the true nature of all phenomena, devoid of all independent self or substance.

Shûnyamûrti (Sanskrit): "the form or manifestation of the void"; traditional epithet of the Buddha, in whom is "incarnate" *shûnyatâ,* ultimate "emptiness", that is, the absence of all definite being or selfhood.

Sub specie aeternitatis (Latin): literally, "under the aspect of eternity", that is, from the point of view of the Absolute.

Sukhâvatî (Sanskrit): "blissful"; in Amidist or Pure Land Buddhism, the Western Paradise into which faithful devotees of Amitabha are believed to be reborn and in which they lead a blissful life until finally entering *Nirvâna.*

Sunnah (Arabic): "custom, usage, way of acting"; in Islam, the norm established by the Prophet Muhammad, including his actions and sayings (see *hadîth*) and serving as a precedent and standard for the behavior of Muslims.

Sûrah (Arabic): a chapter or division of the Koran, the holy book of Islam.

Vaisheshika (Sanskrit): literally, "referring to the distinctions"; Hindu philosophy of nature, including an analysis of the various categories and objects of sensory experience; one of the six orthodox *darshana*s, or perspectives, of classical Hinduism.

Vaishya (Sanskrit): a member of the third of the four Hindu castes, including merchants, craftsmen, farmers; the distinctive qualities of the *vaishya* are honesty, balance, perseverance; see *brâhmana, kshatriya, shûdra.*

Vedânta (Sanskrit): "end or culmination of the Vedas"; one of the major schools of traditional Hindu philosophy, based in part on the Upanishads, esoteric treatises found at the conclusion of the Vedic scriptures; see *advaita*.

Wakan Tanka (Lakota): literally, "Great Sacred" or "Great Mystery", but usually translated "Great Spirit"; the Divine conceived as both impersonal Essence and personal Creator.

Yin-Yang (Chinese): in Chinese tradition, two opposite but complementary forces or qualities, from whose interpenetration the universe and all its diverse forms emerge; *Yin* corresponds to the feminine, the yielding, the moon, and liquidity; *Yang* corresponds to the masculine, the resisting, the sun, and solidity.

Yoga (Sanskrit): literally, "joining, union"; an ensemble of spiritual and psychosomatic techniques intended to bring the soul and body into a state of concentration or meditative focus.

Zâhir (Arabic): the "Outward"; in Islam, *az-Zâhir* is a divine Name, as in the Koranic verse, "He is the First and the Last, the Outward and the Inward" (*Sûrah* "Iron" [57]:3); also used with the meaning "exoteric".

Zâwiyah (Arabic): literally, "corner, nook"; in Sufism, any place of prayer and retreat used by members of a spiritual brotherhood, whether a mosque or a single room.

For a glossary of all key foreign words used in books published by World Wisdom, including metaphysical terms in English, consult:
www.DictionaryofSpiritualTerms.org.
This on-line Dictionary of Spiritual Terms provides extensive definitions, examples and related terms in other languages.

Index

Abraham, the sacrifice of, 9

Absolute, the, 10, 16, 18, 22, 29, 31, 34-35, 39-41, 45-46, 49-50, 53-55, 67, 76-78, 81-82, 90-91, 93-94, 96-97, 102, 104, 106-107, 110-111, 113, 116, 119-122, 125, 127, 129, 131, 137, 139-140, 142-143

action, the exclusivism of, 39

action, the problem of, 41

Adam, 20, 33-34, 44, 56, 80

Adam, the sin of, 33

adulterous woman, the, 9

afterlife, the, 138

alchemy, 56, 66

Algonquins, the, 63-64

American Indians, the spiritual quality of, 60

Amidism, 104-105

Amitabha, 104, 124, 146

Anaximenes of Miletus, 52

animism, polysynthetic, 64

apocalypticism, 70

apocatastasis, 35, 81, 139

apologetics, 107

Apostolic period, the, 85

architecture, "avant-garde", 7

aristocracy, the excesses of, 10

Aristotle, 50-52

Aristotelianism, 104

art criticism, 90

art, Gothic, 6-7

art, Romanesque, 7

art, sacred 7, 27, 43-44, 126, 130-131

artists, modern, 30

arts of divination, the, 7

athanor, 67

atheistic materialism, the success of, 109

Âtmâ, 76, 79, 82, 120, 123, 128, 131, 135, 139

authority, in Western Christianity, 3

Avatâra, 40, 82, 139

Babylonians, the, 8-9

barakah, 43-44, 139

believers, 4, 13, 27, 38, 70, 129

Benedict, Saint, 106

Beyond-Being, 29, 78, 132

bhakti, 37, 48, 140, 142-144

Bible, the, 37, 92, 107, 115-118, 134

Biblical style, 116

biologism, 23

Black Elk (Hehaka Sapa), 65, 68, 69, 71, 81

bodhisattva, 124, 140

Brahma, 140, 143

brâhmana, 40, 140-142, 146

Buddha, 33, 104, 124, 144, 146

Buddhism, 104-105, 124, 140, 142-146

Caesar, 2, 15, 51, 149, 152

Caesar Augustus, 2

Caesar, "divine right" of, 15

calamities, 16, 37, 80

Calumet, rite of the, 67

cardinal points, the, 65-66

caritas, 48, 139-140

Cassian, 106

Catherine of Siena, Saint, 123

sacred arrows, of the Cheyenne, 72
Sacred Pipe, the, 67-68
sages, 8, 23, 30, 46, 49, 51, 65, 116, 120
saints, the, 23-24, 38, 61, 90, 102-103, 108-109, 111
salamanders, 87
salvation, 46-49, 122
Samsâra, 33, 81, 124, 131, 143, 145
Samurai, the, 71
Sanhedrin, the, 116
sannyâsin, 125, 145
Sânkhya, 52, 141, 145
Satori, 136, 145
schisms, 13
science, experimental, 26, 28
science, modern, 24-28, 93, 98, 111, 136
science, Western, 25
scientism, 13-14, 27, 89, 108, 118
scientism, evolutionist, 51
Scriptures, sacred, 129
Scriptures, the, 37, 55, 108, 112, 115-116
secularism, 20
Self, the, 29, 49, 54, 76, 78-79, 81-82, 95, 99, 102, 134, 139, 141, 146
sentiments, the nobility of, 130
serpent, the, 63, 98
Shahâdah, 123, 145
Shakespeare, William, 69, 89, 96
Shamanism, 59, 67, 134
shamans, 25, 68-69
Shinto, 43, 59, 63, 134, 142
Shoshone, 68
shûdra, 140, 146
Shûnya, 82, 124, 146
Silesius, Angelus, 78
sin, absolute, 41

sin, relative, 41
Sioux, the, 62, 66, 70-71
skeptics, 51-52
socialism, demagogic, 51
Socrates, 50-51
Song of Songs, the, 114
Sophists, the, 52
sorcery, 69, 88
Sovereign Good, the, 130
spirits, the discerning of, 43
spiritual life, the, 25, 128, 133
spiritual master, the, 103, 141, 144-145
Sufis, 36, 79
Sufis, the doctrine of, 75
Sufism, 141-142, 145, 147
Sukhâvatî, 16, 146
Sun Dance, the, 67-68, 135
sunnah, 103, 146
supernatural, the, 7, 55, 61, 90, 97, 103
superstition, 87-88, 90
Supreme Being, the, 21, 60
supreme Law, the, 18, 37
Supreme Principle, the, 45, 76
surgery, 136
surrealism, 26, 51
Susanao-o, 63
sweat lodge, the, 67
syllogisms, 51
symbolism, 5, 7, 15, 25, 27, 43, 52, 66, 88, 93, 96-97, 109, 113, 115, 117, 121-122, 124-125, 130, 133
syncretism and eclecticism, 104

Tacitus, 89
Taoists, 105
temporal power, 3
temptations, 102
Ten Commandments, the, 134
Testimony of Unity, the, 123
Thales, 52

Biographical Notes

FRITHJOF SCHUON was born in Basle, Switzerland in 1907, and was the twentieth century's pre-eminent spokesman for the perennialist school of comparative religious thought.

The leitmotif of Schuon's work was foreshadowed in an encounter during his youth with a marabout who had accompanied some members of his Senegalese village to Basle for the purpose of demonstrating their African culture. When Schuon talked with him, the venerable old man drew a circle with radii on the ground and explained: "God is the center; all paths lead to Him." Until his later years Schuon traveled widely, from India and the Middle East to America, experiencing traditional cultures and establishing lifelong friendships with Hindu, Buddhist, Christian, Muslim, and American Indian spiritual leaders.

A philosopher in the tradition of Plato, Shankara, and Eckhart, Schuon was a gifted artist and poet as well as the author of over twenty books on religion, metaphysics, sacred art, and the spiritual path. Describing his first book, *The Transcendent Unity of Religions*, T. S. Eliot wrote, "I have met with no more impressive work in the comparative study of Oriental and Occidental religion", and world-renowned religion scholar Huston Smith has said of Schuon that "the man is a living wonder; intellectually apropos religion, equally in depth and breadth, the paragon of our time". Schuon's books have been translated into over a dozen languages and are respected by academic and religious authorities alike.

More than a scholar and writer, Schuon was a spiritual guide for seekers from a wide variety of religions and backgrounds throughout the world. He died in 1998.

DEBORAH CASEY graduated *magna cum laude* from Indiana University with a bachelor's degree in fine arts. As a student she encountered the writings of Frithjof Schuon and other perennialist authors, and in 1974 she traveled to Switzerland to meet Schuon. Mrs. Casey has been with World Wisdom since 1981, and in her capacity as editor she had the opportunity to meet frequently with Schuon for the publication of many of his books in English translation. Her current responsibilities involve working with other translators and editors on the translation and cataloging of Schuon's correspondence and unpublished papers for the future use of interested readers and scholars.